A HISTORY LOVER'S GUIDE TO
BAR HARBOR

A HISTORY LOVER'S GUIDE TO BAR HARBOR

Brian Armstrong
Foreword by Deborah M. Dyer, Bar Harbor Historical Society

Published by The History Press
Charleston, SC
www.historypress.com

Copyright © 2021 by Brian Armstrong
All rights reserved

Cover photographs provided courtesy of Katahdin Photo Gallery (Steven Bart) and Mike Perlman.

Opposite: Constance "Connie" Ells Armstrong in 1950. *Courtesy of the author.*

First published 2021

Manufactured in the United States

ISBN 9781467147804

Library of Congress Control Number: 2021931126

Notice: The information in this book is true and complete to the best of our knowledge. It is offered without guarantee on the part of the author or The History Press. The author and The History Press disclaim all liability in connection with the use of this book.

All rights reserved. No part of this book may be reproduced or transmitted in any form whatsoever without prior written permission from the publisher except in the case of brief quotations embodied in critical articles and reviews.

This book is dedicated to the memory of my mother, Constance Ells Armstrong (1927–2014).

CONTENTS

Foreword, by Deborah M. Dyer   11
Acknowledgements   13
Introduction   17
Mount Desert   21
Map of the Bar Harbor Historic Buildings and
    Monuments Trail   23

1. The Bar Harbor Wharf (Ells Plaque, Bar Harbor Municipal Pier,
    One Town Pier)   25

2. The Queen and the Princess of Saloons: Lizzie Ford and
    Ada Bearse (Galyn's Restaurant, 17 Main Street)   38

3. The Return of Eden's Prodigal Sons: Herb Redding and
    Smylie Grant Ells (Sherman's Book Store, 56 Main Street)   48

4. Bar Harbor Village Improvement Association and the
    One-Horse Town (Morrison Building, 62 Main Street)   56

5. The Bradley Block (First National Bank, 102 Main Street)   60

6. Bee's Store and Miss Shaw (Bar Harbor Hemporium,
    116 Main Street)   65

Contents

7. The Will of William M. Roberts (Roberts Monument,
    Bar Harbor Village Green) — 70

8. The Car and the Village Green (Village Green Bandstand,
    Village Green, Main and Mount Desert Streets) — 75

9. The Coaster's Checkbook/Ash Graves (Mount Desert Street
    Cemetery, 41 Mount Desert Street) — 81

10. The Church Lady: Elizabeth Higgins (St. Saviour's Episcopal
    Church and Rectory, 41 Mount Desert Street) — 90

11. The Misses Shannon (Ledgelawn Inn,
    66 Mount Desert Street) — 97

12. Oldest Cottage on Mount Desert Street (Stone Throw Cottage Inn
    and Mira Monte Inn, 67 and 69 Mount Desert Street) — 105

13. The Lost Girl of Holland Avenue (Jane Parker House,
    48 Holland Avenue) — 114

14. The Missing Block (Walter Bird House, 10 Holland Avenue) — 122

15. The Music Hall, the Casino and the Way Bak Ball
    (Alonzo Ash House, 6 Summer Street) — 127

16. World War I and the Spanish Influenza (George Edwin Kirk
    American Legion Post 0025, 70 Cottage Street) — 137

17. Pearl Otto Wescott and the Star Theatre (Star Theatre Building,
    44 Cottage Street) — 145

18. Rags to Riches: How Peanut Row Became the Harborside Hotel
    (Whale Watch Building/Clark Coal Company Building,
    55 West Street) — 155

19. The West End Hotel and the Bar Harbor Club
    (Bar Harbor Club, 111 West Street) — 160

Contents

20. Dr. John B. Ells and the OBE (La Rochelle/Bar Harbor Historical Society, 127 West Street) — 167

21. The Corner of Eden and West Streets (DeGregoire Green and Plaque, West and Eden Streets Corner) — 172

22. The Coughs and the Atlantic Oakes (Sonny Cough Plaque by the Atlantic Eyrie Lodge, 6 Norman Road) — 177

Afterword — 189
Notes — 191
Bibliography — 201
About the Author — 205

FOREWORD

It is a privilege to be asked by Brian Armstrong to write the foreword to this book. Many of the stories have appeared in the Bar Harbor Historical Society newsletters, as Brian was kind enough to share his knowledge with our members.

Brian is quite a history buff and comes rightly by it through his relatives. His grandfather, the late Dr. John B. Ells, was among a group known as the "wharf rats," as they were always at the Bar Harbor Town Pier greeting people and telling stories. Therefore, the town pier was dedicated as the Ells Pier on August 15, 1973. "Doc" Ells worked diligently to bring ships to Bar Harbor, entertain the sailors and arrange for townspeople to tour the vessels, many of which were British ships. In appreciation of his efforts, Dr. Ells was awarded the OBE (Order of the British Empire) by Queen Elizabeth and Prince Philip in 1955 as the "Greeter of the Fleet." The Bar Harbor Historical Society was very pleased that Brian's cousin Sheree Castonguay loaned the OBE to them, and it is on display at La Rochelle.

As curator of the Bar Harbor Historical Society since 1989, Brian's stories and donations were priceless to me. These stories about Bar Harbor are some that the public has never heard, as they have been handed down from generation to generation in Brian's family. I hope that people enjoy reading this book about "Old Bar Harbor" as much as I know I will.

—Deborah M. Dyer
Bar Harbor curator/historian

ACKNOWLEDGEMENTS

The key person to acknowledge for this book is my mother, Constance "Connie" Ells Armstrong, who created the seed for my historical research. Her wonderful stories that she told me as a child provided an inspiration for this book about Bar Harbor that goes deeper than the usual historical overview.

My father, Quentin Armstrong, fostered my love of buildings, which helped me understand the landscape of Bar Harbor during the last 150 years. These surviving structures provide a window to the past. He also stimulated my interest in history from a young age with trips to the Metropolitan Museum of Art in New York City, dinnertime discussions about lost empires like the Hittites and Rome and his history magazines and books.

Debbie Dyer was my frequent collaborator and friend over the last thirty years through her work with the Bar Harbor Historical Society. She has always been there to answer the tough questions, point me in the right direction for research and provide that local connection to the people that my mother mentioned in her stories. She provided me the forum to present articles through the Bar Harbor Historical Society newsletter for many years. Without her encouragement and help, I would not have had the opportunity to develop my historical writing and expand my knowledge of nineteenth- and twentieth-century Bar Harbor.

Other local Bar Harbor residents who have helped me with this book were Anna Burns, John Clark, Dickie Cough, Richard Duperey, Dick and Barbara Fox, Sheldon and John Goldthwait, Terese Miller, Paul Richardson,

Acknowledgements

Kim Swan and Tom Testa. Jennifer L. McWain, former assistant clerk of Bar Harbor, provided so much valuable information about my family. Leon Hubbard provided interesting stories when I spoke to him each summer at his sports store. Jack Ells must be thanked for all the Smylie Ells stories. Phil Cunningham would be happy that I included the Bar Harbor Village Improvement Association (BHVIA) in the book. Sally Higgins Pim in the United Kingdom and David Higgins in Maine provided great information about the Higgins family of Locust Lane.

The staff and the online services of the Hancock County Registry of Deeds and the Registry of Probate were a great resource for this book. Google was important due to their scanning of several books about Bar Harbor that had valuable information concerning businesses and people in the town. Ancestry.com provided census, directories, military records, wills and death records.

Emery DeBeck has been a Maine history hero for me for many years. He always seems to find very interesting, obscure pieces of history, such as the hidden birth of Ellen Ash in southern Maine; information about my great-great-grandfather's mistress, Eliza Ann Crabtree; and a newspaper item recording the construction of houses by Alonzo, Orlando and Nathan Ash in 1879. Although these items seem unimportant, they became key parts of the puzzle to accurately chronicle the history of the area.

Sherman's Book Store was always there every summer with a new book about Bar Harbor to help me better understand the people, events and places that have molded the history of the area. I would also like to thank all those authors who have written books about Bar Harbor. You may not think people constantly refer to your books, but I can assure you I do. My favorite Bar Harbor book is Ruth Ann Hill's *Discovering Old Bar Harbor and Acadia National Park*, which uses newspapers and other unusual sources, a great early map of Eden (Bar Harbor) from the 1850s and a creative layout.

My history professors at American University in Washington, D.C., always stressed that the best historical research and books were those about a subject that had not been written about and about interesting people who have been ignored. I have followed their advice during the writing of this book.

Digitized Bar Harbor newspapers were a key research tool for this book. My extensive use of the newspaper archive of *Bar Harbor Mount Desert Herald* and the *Bar Harbor Record* is a tribute to their editor, Helen M. Smith, who purchased the *Bar Harbor Record* in 1893 and owned the paper for twenty years. A third key newspaper, the *Bar Harbor Times*, was the main town newspaper

Acknowledgements

for one hundred years. I first began viewing Bar Harbor newspaper archives on microfiche in the basement of the Jesup Memorial Library in the 1980s and later through digitized and indexed versions through Newspaperarchive.com. These newspapers from 1881 to 1968 provide detailed information about every aspect of Bar Harbor life during the season and the rest of the year. These newspaper pages were the key resource for this book and a window to the past.

Thank you to my wife for being my companion during my Maine trips and her encouragement and interest in my historical writing about the town and its people.

And finally, I thank Harvard Higgins, who back in the late 1970s showed me the location of the graves of my great-great-grandparents Captain Benjamin Ash and Maria (aka Mariah) Higgins Ash in the Mount Desert Street Cemetery. Like a high priest in an old Universal Studios mummy movie, he led the eighteen-year-old novice to the important graves. This was the moment when I connected fully with the history of my family and Bar Harbor. Since that time, every visit includes a visit to the graves and the other wonderful surviving artifacts. I hope my journey each year can be shared with the audience of this book. You have probably walked by many of these buildings and monuments numerous times, and I hope that I can create a connection to the location with a story so that history can come alive and long-gone people and events will be remembered and valued.

INTRODUCTION

When I decided to write a book about Bar Harbor, I wanted to make sure it would not be a rehash of what had already been published about the town. I love the town so much, and when any new book about Bar Harbor is published, I buy it from Sherman's Book Store when I visit each summer. Unlike most of the people who have written about the town, my family has deep roots that go back to the founding of Eden (Bar Harbor). I constantly search in the new published books for new information about the town but usually find the same narrative. I even go on eBay and buy old smelly copies of classic Bar Harbor books that are no longer in print, like the 1948 Richard W. Hale book. These books have some historical nuggets, but they lack detail except when discussing the summer colony.

My wife told me that if I write a book about Bar Harbor, I need to retell all my mother's wonderful stories about the town. She was a great storyteller before Alzheimer's disease silenced her a few years ago, and I have included these stories to restore her voice. As a child, I was an eager listener who constantly asked her to retell the stories of long-gone events and people. She grew up in the town as the daughter of an overachiever, Dr. John B. Ells, who pulled himself out of poverty to graduate as a dentist from University of Pennsylvania and become the political and civic dynamo for the next sixty years in his beloved town. I was fortunate enough to have known him as a child and enjoyed his self-deprecating sense of humor. I share these stories not to promote my family but instead to ensure that these wonderful stories that provide valuable historical information are not lost. Many Bar Harbor

Introduction

families have similar stories that have been passed down; however, I don't know them. Maybe this book will motivate others to record their families' stories before they are lost.

The plan of the book is a trail in the town that connects existing buildings and monuments with historical people and events. I use the 2017 Chapter 125, Land Use Ordinance, Appendix A of Historic Properties in the Design Review Overlay District of the Town Code and my own knowledge of historic buildings in Bar Harbor as a guide to existing important historic buildings. Buildings are listed with their historic name, current name, address and year built. This is how I experience the town when I visit it each year, and I wanted to share this experience with others. Many of the locations are linked to stories that have been passed down to me. I hope that the stories will stimulate an appreciation for these buildings and monuments.

I started the trail with the wharf and the Porcupine Islands since this is still the view that I look forward to each summer. It is also the view that my grandfather, in all types of weather and ages of his life, experienced daily to recharge his batteries. It was a fitting honor when the town named the wharf that he loved so much for him in the early 1970s after he passed.

My mother was a quiet feminist who was always interested in books, movies and TV shows that showed strong women in a positive way. I have provided profiles of several interesting women who have been overlooked in most books. It amazed me for years that the Misses Shannon (Mary Jr. and Mary Sr.) have been neglected in discussions about the summer colony. Other key women such as Lizzie Ford, Ada Bearse, Pearl Wescott, Isa Dora Shaw, Elizabeth Higgins, Mariam Roberts and others are featured in the book.

Since much of what has been written about Bar Harbor usually features dead white men, I discuss a few prominent African Americans, such as Captain Frederick Allen and Hanley Mathews Davis, who hosted the Colored Folks Annual Dance in Bar Harbor for at least twenty years. My former boss Galen Leek once told me that he was one of those invisible African American workers who came to Bar Harbor every summer. His father, Goodridge Leek, who emigrated from New Brunswick, Canada, in 1905, was a truck driver for a coal company in Bangor and owned his own home. Galen later had a successful career working for the FAA and owned an IT contracting firm with Clarence Jones in Washington, D.C., Kajax Engineering, Inc. I have not included profiles of Native Americans in this book since *Indians of Eden* by McBride and Prins provides excellent information about this important group.

Introduction

Forgotten venues such as the Music Hall, Hapworth & Burr Hall, Star Theatre, the Dreamwood and the Casino are discussed. These venues were so popular that during most of their existence, an address in a newspaper advertisement was not necessary since everyone knew their locations. Except for the Casino and Dreamwood, these venues have not even been mentioned in other books about Bar Harbor.

Bar Harbor's huge hotels, cottages and private homes are featured as lost and surviving connections to the past. The discovery of the extensive recycling of lumber from large razed hotels reveals that these buildings live on in the surviving cottages and homes that benefited from their fine local wood. When you see the beauty of these surviving buildings and realize that many were just a few feet away from being destroyed by the Fire of 1947, you realize how blessed the town of Eden (Bar Harbor) has been for several hundred years of its existence. The people and the town have survived the loss of their men and women at war, mariners lost at sea, deaths from the Spanish influenza of 1918, the destruction of the Fire of 1947 and the effects of the severe weather to thrive as a tourist mecca.

One of the common threads that comes through in these stories is how people took care of one another in the old days. If you lived in a family and were lucky to have made money, you took care of the less fortunate members of the family through adopting the children they were incapable of raising, providing shelter and money for food and taking care of those who were physically or mentally incapacitated. If you were a rich visitor, you left a house to your caretaker in your will, you encouraged and helped bright local children to succeed and you provided money to construct local buildings that benefited the community. I also learned how people with no more than a sixth-grade education made a living and made sure that their children went to college to better their lives.

I hope the reader of this book enjoys this journey through Bar Harbor history as much as I have over the last sixty years.

MOUNT DESERT

Mount Desert. When you hear the name spoken, what does it call up in your mind? Just what it should: a picture of Champlain sailing the harbor in the dim and misty past and first catching sight of a barren chain of mountains rising from the bosom of a rocky island. He named it the "Ile of the Desert Mountains" or "Mount Desert." Surely it is a fitting and proper name for our island home.

There is an unexplained peace and quiet on Mount Desert. People come here and return year after year.

> *The whole island has a romantic history and dreams of bygone years still cling to the hills and meadows. Where could be found more beauty, more charm, more mystery, than on the Island of Mount Desert?*
> —Jane Wheeler Parker, Bar Harbor High School class of 1916

> *You may live in Bar Harbor, but I still live in Eden.*
> —Melinda Brewer after the name of town was changed from Eden to Bar Harbor, 1918

> *As Bar Harbor receded in the distance it looked like a dream island rising from the sea, the same pale blue as Capri seen from Naples but a far more beautiful shape! There's nothing to compare with it!*
> —journals of Marian Lawrence Peabody, courtesy of Gertrude Lawrence McCue, Bar Harbor Historical Society

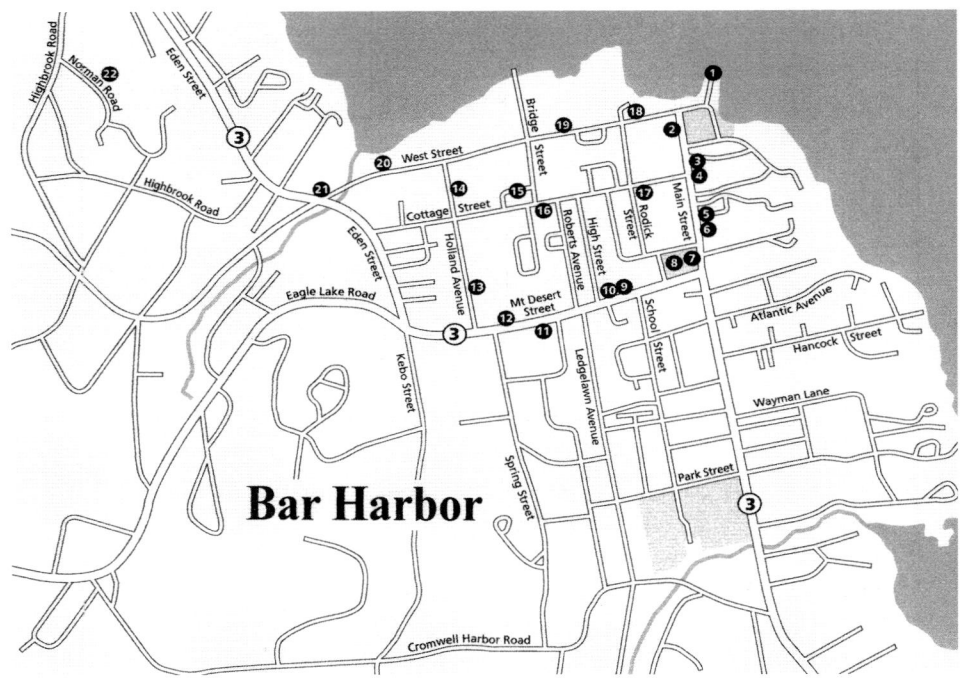

Map of the Bar Harbor Historic Buildings and Monuments Trail. *Courtesy of the author.*

MAP OF THE BAR HARBOR HISTORIC BUILDINGS AND MONUMENTS TRAIL

1. Ells Plaque (Bar Harbor Municipal Pier, One Town Pier)
2. Galyn's Restaurant (17 Main Street)
3. Sherman's Book Store (56 Main Street)
4. Morrison Building (62 Main Street)
5. First National Bank (102 Main Street)
6. Bar Harbor Hemporium (116 Main Street)
7. Roberts Monument (Village Green, Main Street)
8. Bandstand (Village Green, Main and Mount Desert Street)
9. Ash Graves, Mount Desert Street Cemetery (41 Mount Desert Street)
10. St. Saviour's Episcopal Church and Rectory (41 Mount Desert Street)
11. Ledgelawn Inn (66 Mount Desert Street)
12. Stone Throw Cottage Inn and Mira Monte Inn (67 and 69 Mount Desert Street)
13. Jane Parker House (48 Holland Avenue)
14. Walter Bird House (10 Holland Avenue)
15. Alonzo Ash House (6 Summer Street)
16. George Edwin Kirk American Legion Post (70 Cottage Street)
17. Star Theatre Building (44 Cottage Street)
18. Whale Watch Building (55 West Street)
19. Bar Harbor Club (111 West Street)
20. La Rochelle, Bar Harbor Historical Society (127 West Street)
21. DeGregoire Green and Plaque (corner Eden and West Streets)
22. Sonny Cough Plaque (Atlantic Eyrie Lodge) (6 Norman Road)

Chapter 1

THE BAR HARBOR WHARF

ELLS PLAQUE
BAR HARBOR MUNICIPAL PIER, ONE TOWN PIER

Any discussion of the history of the wharf/municipal pier in Bar Harbor must begin with Tobias Roberts and Captain Charles Deering. Tobias Roberts owned the land by the waterfront and established the first hotel, Agamont House (1855), when he saw the first wave of visitors in the 1850s. He then developed the first wharf, which provided the docking for Captain Deering's steamboat. Once Roberts and Deering created the transportation portal to the island, the rest, as they say, is history. In 1853, Deering opened a hotel on Main Street, the Deering House. In 1866, Roberts convinced the town of Eden (Bar Harbor) to build Main Street next to his hotel.

Roberts and Deering worked together on the plan that radically transformed the wharf area. The Maine state legislature gave Roberts permission to build the wharf in 1867 and to extend it in 1872. When he renovated the existing wharf in 1873, forty feet was added to the wharf, costing $6,000. This wharf was known as the Steamship Wharf.

Then they hatched a plan that made them both rich and exponentially expanded the number of steamships coming to Bar Harbor. Due to the fear that Eastern Railroad Company had about Boston and Maine Railroad getting the business in Bar Harbor, Roberts was able to sell his wharf, which was possibly worth $20,000 at most, for $33,500 or, as some sources note, $38,500. The irony is that this purchase and other financial mistakes led to the sale of Eastern Railroad Company to the Boston and Maine Railroad later that decade.

The Ells plaque (stop no. 1) at the end of the Bar Harbor Municipal Pier (wharf) in the 1980s. *Courtesy of the author.*

Although travelers from Boston and New York could reach Bar Harbor by ship, other travelers dependent on the railroads required the last leg of the journey to be by steamship. For local travelers visiting or providing services for the island and those coming from Philadelphia and other non-coastal locations, these steamers were essential.

In 1883, the Eastern Railroad Company was granted the right to expand the wharf. After the expansion, the Maine Central Railroad bought the wharf in 1884 and made it its docking location, which expanded the tourist industry in Bar Harbor. Near the end of 1884, Eastern Railroad Company leased its tracks to the Boston and Maine Railroad, and they were incorporated into its Portland Division.

In 1884, Maine Central Railroad changed travel to the island by establishing the ferry from Bar Harbor to Hancock at the end of the train track. The railroad established the 161-foot *Sappho* as the boat to carry people to and from Bar Harbor three times a day, competing with three steamer lines that carried people from Boston and New York to the island.

The *Sappho* was known for its "spacious saloons and elegant staterooms"[1] during the forty-minute ride to Bar Harbor from the mainland.

The largest disaster during the steamer era concerning the Maine Central Railroad ferry occurred on August 6, 1899, when two hundred "excursionists from Bangor and other points" fell into the water fifteen feet below when the ferry gangplank gave way at the dock at Ferry Point in the town of Hancock.[2] Twenty victims drowned, "shut in on all sides, having no avenue of escape, clutched one another and sank in groups before the work of rescue could be begun."[3] Many unconscious persons were rescued alive from the water "by ropes and manpower" and "revived with great difficulty."[4]

The wharf was called the Maine Central Railroad Wharf from 1884 to 1931 when it was owned by the railroad. During this era, a new terminal was built with a larger waiting room, a ticket office, freight buildings and express offices on the dock. In the early twentieth century, schooners declined, private yachts increased, boat rental business increased and passenger steamers were popular. By 1921, the Maine Central Railroad Wharf was five hundred feet long with a nine-foot depth of terminal at low tide.

After the end of the steamer era, the wharf, which was made of wood pilings, was decaying. The town planned to replace the old docks with a new Municipal Pier and to develop Agamont Park at the end of Main Street in the 1930s. Dr. John B. Ells was elected chairman of the board of selectmen and pushed through the funding for construction of the granite block structure.

The wharf was renovated and expanded again during World War II to accommodate the U.S. and English ships that came to Bar Harbor. This renovation began when Dr. Ells talked the town into turning over the town pier to the U.S. Navy for one dollar.

Shortly after the navy took over, Dr. Ells tried to visit his beloved wharf and was cut off by a chain-link fence and an armed guard. Ells devised a clever plan to continue his wharf visits by being appointed harbormaster and then invoking Maine law notifying the naval officials that the "town-owned moorings were not safe for the naval ships to tie up to unless they were inspected."[5] An inspection in those days required the expense of either hauling the mooring ashore or sending deep-sea divers in pressurized helmets and suits to the ocean bottom to check each and every link in the mooring chains of every naval vessel. Within twenty-four hours, Dr. Ells was once again allowed his nightly walks around the pier to "inspect," and the formal inspection was deemed not necessary. Throughout the war, he was the only civilian allowed free access to the pier.

After the war, the operation of the wharf was returned to the town, and it was known as the municipal pier. Dr. Ells continued to get navy ships to come to Bar Harbor every summer. During the years after the war, he was able to get hundreds of warships, including the battleship *Missouri*, to visit the town. In 1952, the navy honored Dr. Ells with a Navy Citation. He was also awarded the Order of the British Empire (OBE) from Queen Elizabeth II in 1955 for his assistance to the British navy during the war. He was said to have greeted twenty thousand British and American naval officers and one hundred thousand sailors, providing "dinners, dances, bus rides, tours, boxing matches, swimming parties and other activities during his years as Chairman of the Warships Committee."

In the early 1960s, "some little snot-nosed kid" in the navy informed Ells that they were unable to provide Bar Harbor with a ship that year for the Fourth of July.[6] Dr. Ells called his close friend Senator Margaret Chase Smith in Washington, D.C., who he knew as "Maggie."[7] A few minutes after the call, he got a call back from her office with plans to provide "not one but two naval vessels, a destroyer and a submarine."[8]

In December 1971, Dr. Ells died, and Bar Harbor Municipal Pier was renamed the Dr. John B. Ells Pier in the early 1970s with the help of Albert

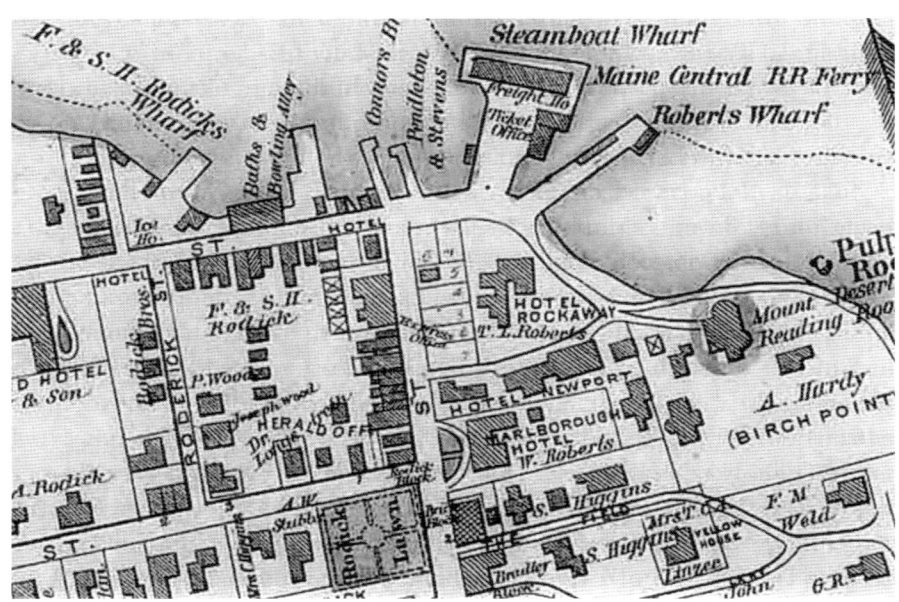

Map of Bar Harbor Wharf in the 1880s. *Courtesy of the Bar Harbor Historical Society.*

Steamboat Wharf in the late 1880s. *Courtesy of Southwest Harbor Library.*

Cunningham. On August 15, 1973, a plaque was dedicated at the end of the right side of the Bar Harbor Municipal Pier reading: "The Dr. John B. Ells Pier. Dedicated to the memory of John B. Ells, D.D.S., 1890–1971, a civic and political leader, devoted to this pier, the navies of the world and to the visitors to this pier. Recipient of the Order of the British Empire."

Senator Margaret Chase Smith wrote in a letter that "no greater honor could be extended to John B. Ells's memory than the naming of the pier for him" since "he had great pride and love for Bar Harbor and his fellow citizens."[9] His effort made Bar Harbor a "favorite with the Navy" because of his "warm and generous welcome and hospitality."

William S. Cohen, member of the U.S. House of Representatives from Maine's second district (and future U.S. senator and secretary of defense), entered in the congressional record on October 1, 1973: "The plaque now installed at the end of the John B. Ells Pier stands as a monument to this remarkable man. This recognition will also bring back many pleasant memories to those who had the good fortune to be in Bar Harbor during Dr. Ells's lifetime."

THE ROBERTS WHARF

After selling the old wharf, Tobias Roberts's son Tobias Roberts Jr. built a wharf in 1883 to the right of the original wharf that today would be located between the municipal pier and to the left of the Bar Harbor Inn pier. The Roberts Wharf was originally associated with the people who visited the Roberts family hotels, the Rockaway (1870) and the Newport House (1869).

In 1885, Tobias Roberts Jr. wanted to expand the wharf to 250 feet from the high water with a turn to the right to dock steamships. Adjoining landowner George W. Dillingham, the successful publisher of novels, took him to court, claiming the wharf expansion would "materially obstruct access" to his lot between Roberts's land and Hardy's Point (Birch Point, 1868). Tobias Roberts Sr. was also against the wharf expansion. The case was dismissed without prejudice, and Roberts completed his expansion. An 1895 map called the wharf the Roberts Wharf, and later it became the Bangor and Bar Harbor Steam Ship Company Wharf. There was enough room between the two large wharfs to fit a steamship.

Here is a description of the steamship excursion from Boston to the Roberts Wharf in the 1890s:

> *The* Olivette *leaves Boston every Tuesday, Thursday and Saturday, at 6 P.M., and arrives at Bar Harbor the following morning at 7. Returning, leaves Bar Harbor every Monday, Wednesday and Friday, at 6 P.M. The fare by this line is first-class, one way, $5.00, excursion, $9.00; second class, $3.00. Staterooms, $2, $3, and $4, according to size. The smaller stateroom accommodated two persons, while the larger rooms accommodated three or four persons traveling together. The* Olivette *offered all the conveniences and comforts of a first-class hotel.*[10]

The Eastern Steamship Company was founded in 1901 by the Wall Street financier C.W. Morse by consolidating six small New England coastwise lines. It provided service between New York and New England and later branched into winter cruises to Florida. Eastern Steamship Company leased the wharf in Bar Harbor from the Roberts family and began using the wharf soon after being established. In 1906, they built a new wharf that was "somewhat larger than the old," and while it was the same length, it was "wider at the end."[11] The buildings were "ample for all the business of the company and included waiting rooms, toilets, freight rooms, etc."[12] The cost of the new wharf was $20,000.[13]

The Eastern Steamship Company merged in 1911 with the Metropolitan Steamship Company and the Maine Steamship Company. It appears that the Roberts family retained ownership of the property until 1912, when they sold other land, including "Hardy's point," to the Maine Central Railroad. By 1913, this wharf was primarily involved with the activities of the Eastern Steamship Company to Rockland (steamship *J.T. Morse* from 1904 to 1931), Maine Coast Transportation boats from Boston to Maine coast ports and Winter Harbor transportation for local traffic.

The Eastern Steamship Company was forced to declare bankruptcy in 1914. Three years later, it reemerged, reorganized as Eastern Steamship Lines, with the Yarmouth Line and a wharf that was five hundred feet long with a nine-foot depth. The present-day Royal Caribbean Cruise Line is in part the corporate descendant of the Eastern Steamship Company. The Eastern Steamship Wharf was razed in the 1930s. The beach area between the municipal pier and the Bar Harbor Inn is the area where this important wharf stood for over fifty years.

THE STEEL PIER

The Mount Desert Reading Room, which was designed by William Ralph Emerson, was built in 1887 by the Oasis Club. A pier was also built before 1888, and it was used by the yacht club, where "a number of crack yachts for New York and Boston from the Eastern Yacht Club" were "gayly dressed with bunting lying at anchor in the harbor."[14] The Mount Desert Reading Room and the wharf south of two large piers was a jointly maintained station for the New York, the Easton and the Seawanhaka-Corinthian Yacht Clubs.

The original pier was destroyed in a storm in 1898, and a massive 230-foot-long steel pier replaced it and opened in 1902. The Steel Pier was a famous Bar Harbor landmark and was pictured in guidebooks, brochures and postcards for several decades.

Vincent C. Messer provided the following detailed description of the pier in his book *A History of the Bar Harbor Inn*:

> *The pattern of the piers steel work, somewhat reminiscent of the steelwork on the Eiffel Tower which was built about a decade earlier resulted in an elegant structure which complemented Emerson's Mount Desert Reading Room design, served a practical purpose to boaters, and provided others a space to stroll and drink tea on the pier's upper deck.*[15]

Roberts Wharf in background and Steel Pier in foreground, late 1800s. *Courtesy of Southwest Harbor Library.*

The Mount Desert Reading Room became the center of social activities during the summers before World War I.[16] In 1910, President William H. Taft was welcomed there upon his arrival in the village near the Steel Pier.

The Oasis Club ended in 1922, and the clubhouse and pier were sold to the Maine Central Railroad, which leased them to the Bar Harbor Yacht Club from 1924 to 1932. In 1933, the building became the Shore Club, started by hotel owners for their guests to use. During World War II, the navy leased the building. After the war, the building was sold to Bar Harbor Hotel Corporation in 1948 and reopened in 1950 with a wing added. The hotel was called the Bar Harbor Motor Inn for several years before it received its current name, the Bar Harbor Inn. The Steel Pier was torn down in 1935 because it was "rusted and worn." It was located several yards south of today's pier for the schooner *Margaret Todd*.

WHARF TRAGEDIES

In the 1920s, Jack Ells (John B. Ells Jr.) was playing on the ice near the shore by the wharf and began to float out to sea on a large piece of ice. His father and other men frantically got a boat and rowed out to rescue him before he fell into the cold winter waters of Frenchman Bay. Other young people were not so lucky with the bay's cold tidal waters.

On April 9, 1947, one of the most infamous stories concerning the wharf occurred. It was a Wednesday evening, and five friends went out and concluded their night with a quick drive by the wharf. The road surface was "glazed with ice," and the car, driven by Elliott "Squeak" Sawyer, slid on the ice and ended up in the water at the end of the wharf.[17] The driver, who opened the door as the car went over the edge, and one of the passengers in the front seat, Barbara Curry, a teacher at Emerson grammar school, got out and swam to the pier to safety. George "Bud" Dolliver Jr. (twenty-three), also in the front seat, was able to get out of the car but drowned clutching the fender guide. The two people in the backseat, Carroll Frost Jr. (twenty-three) of Bar Harbor and Elinor Talbot (twenty-two) of West Haven, Connecticut, also drowned in the April waters of Frenchman Bay. Emergency people called to the scene reported the frustrating glow of the lights of the car in the twenty-five feet of water off the wharf as they tried to save the passengers.

Dolliver's mother had a premonition that Wednesday night shortly before the accident, and when she heard the sirens, she knew something awful had happened. Mothers told children the story as a cautionary tale that was revisited after the 1969 Chappaquiddick incident, where Ted Kennedy said he survived the accident by opening the door as the car went off the bridge.

Another local tragedy in the Frenchman Bay area involved eighteen-year-old Richard McKay, who drowned on August 8, 1949. His fishing boat *Lillian* capsized about midnight when a strong wind hit the boat and the boat capsized due to a lost rudder. Richard Rehlander, twenty-one, who was with McKay, managed "to swim to Bald Porcupine Island in the darkness and was picked up by a lobsterman who dropped him on the Shore Path near his home."[18] Since Rehlander "suffered from exposure and exhaustion," it "took some time" before he could provide information about the accident.[19] A U.S. Coast Guard plane, a plane from the Bar Harbor Airport, a Coast Guard cutter and several fishing craft searched all day on August 9 but only found the boat on Turtle Island.

View of the Porcupine Islands from the Bar Harbor Municipal Pier (wharf), 1950s. *Courtesy of the author.*

Robert was the son of Ambrose John McKay, an immigrant from New Brunswick, Canada, who came to Bar Harbor in 1923 to work for Green and Copp Company (successor to Green and Reynolds Company) as a metal worker. McKay later opened his own roofing, sheet metal work and radiator-servicing business. He and his wife, Mary Stella Landry McKay, had six children who attended Bar Harbor's public schools.

Robert's older brother Charles Raymond McKay became one of Bar Harbor's prominent members of the greatest generation, serving in the U.S. Navy during World War II from 1943 to 1946 as a deep-sea diver first class on the USS *Clytie* AS 26 and the USS *Coucal* ASR 8 at Pearl Harbor, Australia, Borneo, Japan (Hiroshima, Hiro-Was Kure, Sadebo), Okinawa and the Philippines.

His diving duties during the Bikini atomic bomb testing impacted McKay for the rest of his life. He experienced radiation exposure in October 1945 at Hiroshima and in July and August 1946 diving at Operations Crossroads, following the Bikini atomic bomb tests Able (uranium) and Baker (plutonium). McKay witnessed the detonation of the test bombs with the huge mushroom clouds and later entered the bomb site at Bikini Lagoon.[20] He saw dead and injured test animals on the decks of several

Charles (Ray) McKay in navy diving gear, 1945. *Courtesy of the McKay family.*

of the ninety fully armed and equipped ships in the target area before diving to recover testing equipment. McKay was told while diving in one of the test sites that the radiation dose marker on his dive suit showed his exposure to radiation was too hot and that he had to surface immediately. He continued to dive for another few weeks in the area before being transferred out, which he felt saved his life.

In 1978, McKay was diagnosed with colon cancer and was treated and recovered after five years. He later became Maryland state commander, legislative liaison, District of Columbia, for the National Association of Atomic Veterans (NAAV) from 1983 to 2002 and fought for recognition of radiation-induced diseases and fair compensation for the atomic (radiated) veterans and their widows. Many of the atomic vets suffered from various cancers, heart conditions, immune system deficiencies, peripheral neuropathy, respiratory problems, depression and other ailments. Even with all his life success raising a family with Venessa Hall McKay, working for Dupont Company and his work with atomic vets, the tragic death of his younger brother Richard was always a topic of great sadness to Ray until his death at the age of ninety-two in 2018.

Although the clothes, the customs, the food and the technology have changed, the wharf, the ocean and the Porcupine Islands are constant gems still enjoyed today as they were when Tobias Roberts built his first wharf. The power of the ocean cannot be ignored, as the tragic stories have shown; however, the waters of Frenchman Bay and the Atlantic Ocean are also the gift that made Bar Harbor prosper and have importance.

Lost West Street: For over a century, various pleasure boat companies, fish markets and other businesses were located near the wharf on West Street. Pleasure boat companies included Jacob Suminsby, Connors Brothers, W.R. Pendleton, Asa Hodgkins, Dirigo Boating Company (R.H. Kellam), Jordan Benson, F.B. Hayes, Charles Parker and Frenchman's Bay Boating Company. Fish markets were provided by the Hodgkins family, H.D. Wakefield, Lewis William Dolliver, Edward McKay, H.A. Perry (Central Fish Market), William H. Reynolds and Paul Sablich. Other businesses included Nickerson, Spratt and Greeley, Fifield & Joy, Fish Net Market and Restaurant, North Atlantic Packing Company and Harp Museum. Stewman's Lobster Pound and new buildings are located on this part of West Street today.

Bonus Historical Sites: The Shore Path includes many wonderful vistas of the Porcupine Islands and Frenchman Bay, as well as the two Egg Rock Battery ten-inch Rodman cannons, Pulpit Rock, Balance Rock, Grant Park and coastal cottages. An area near the wharf, the Field, includes Bass Cottage (1885) and Ullikana (1885).

Chapter 2

THE QUEEN AND THE PRINCESS OF SALOONS: LIZZIE FORD AND ADA BEARSE

GALYN'S RESTAURANT
17 MAIN STREET

Although most of the country considers Prohibition to be a weird experiment that lasted from 1920 to 1933, Maine's experience with prohibiting the sale and consumption of alcohol goes back many more years to 1851, when the first state prohibition occurred. In fact, the concept of prohibition was inspired by Neal Dow, mayor of Portland. His "Maine Law" was a model that the Woman's Christian Temperance Union and other prohibition groups used as their goal for national prohibition.

Several successful saloons existed in Bar Harbor near the wharf area even though alcohol was illegal to sell in Maine in the late 1800s and early 1900s. Some of these saloons were located near what today is Agamont Park. As with Prohibition in the 1920s, Bar Harbor authorities had neither the interest nor resources to actively enforce these laws. Zealous individuals or government entities would periodically pursue violators with legal actions to curtail this activity, which rarely could be sustained for more than a few years before returning to the status quo.

Though men dominated the illegal liquor trade in the late 1890s and early twentieth century in Bar Harbor, two women, Lizzie Ford and her daughter Ada Bearse, were at the center of the illegal liquor trade until the end of Prohibition in 1933. Lizzie was queen since she was actively involved with selling liquor at her own tippling houses. Ada was princess since she benefited from the liquor fortunes of first her mother and then her husband, Dan Herlihy, without ever having to sell a bottle or drink. Ada would also

17 Main Street (stop no. 2), the only surviving former wharf saloon building, Galyn's Restaurant. *Courtesy of the author.*

briefly carry the torch for one of Dan's biggest achievements after he died in the early 1930s: his nightclub, the Dreamwood.

Lizzie Ford was born on June 12, 1850, in Murrays Island, Prince Edward Island. She arrived in Boston in September 1870, and her daughter Ada May Bearse was born on December 12, 1870. The parents listed on her birth record were Captain George A. Bearse and Elizabeth Reynolds, with a residence in Gloucester. The thirty-three-year-old single sea captain/fisherman George Bearse was living with his seventy-year-old mother and thirty-nine-year-old brother, Benjamin, in Gloucester, according to the 1870 census. Captain Bearse must have ventured to Prince Edward Island during one of his voyages and met Lizzie Reynolds. Either her family or the Bearse family paid for Lizzie's passage from Prince Edward Island to Boston. By 1880, the couple were married and living at 8 Trask Street, Gloucester, and her name was Lizzie N. Bearse. They had a second daughter, Bethena Bearse, in 1877, and one other child who died before Captain Bearse passed away on March 26, 1882.

Lizzie's sister Annie Reynolds came to the United States in 1873 and was married on April 28, 1881, to Walter Howard Spooner from Scituate. Spooner was a machinist when they married but soon prospered in his career and became a treasurer of an investment company, a broker and a director of copper mines and other investments. He also owned one thousand shares of stock in the Butte Central Copper Mining Company, various properties in Boston and other valuable assets. Sometime after the death of Captain Bearse, Walter and Annie Spooner took Ada Bearse into their household in Dorchester, where she lived for almost twenty years in affluent Boston society.

Walter H. Spooner divorced Annie and married Flora Baker, a stenographer, in 1899. After the divorce, Annie continued to live with their son Walter Jr. and Ada in Boston. She listed her spouse in directories as Walter H. Spooner for over three decades after his death in 1909.

On September 3, 1885, the widow Lizzie Bearse married Captain Preston W. Kelley in Gloucester. Kelley, a schooner captain, frequently traveled from Bar Harbor to the Boston area and may have met her during one of his stops in Gloucester, where she owned a rooming house. It was the second marriage for both Kelley and Lizzie. The couple moved to Maine not long after the wedding.

Three and a half years later, Captain Kelley filed for divorce in Hancock, Maine. Since Lizzie was the defendant in the divorce, she most likely committed adultery or deserted her husband. After the divorce, Lizzie moved to Bar Harbor. When her daughter Ada Bearse came to visit in March 1894, the first newspaper notice on March 15 called her mother Lizzie N. Kelley, and the second on March 22 called her Lizzie N. Ford. This shows that she was known as Lizzie N. Kelley from the time of her divorce in 1889 until 1892 or early 1893, when she married P.W. Ford. When Patrick married Lizzie, he was in his early twenties and she was at least forty years old.

Ford had been arrested for a liquor charge at his property on West Street in 1892. He had his new wife manage his saloon in his absence. Her two indictments in early 1893 for liquor violations called her Lizzie N. Ford, which was proof of her third marriage to Patrick W. Ford prior to the arrest.

Lizzie's daughter Ada was very bright and excelled in school in Massachusetts while living in Dorchester with Lizzie's sister. She received additional educational and cultural advantages living with the Spooners since she became a very brilliant woman who collected books about English history, literature, biography and art at an early age. She graduated from Boston College of Osteopathy (later called the Massachusetts College of Osteopathy), established an osteopathy practice as Dr. Bearse in Boston and was secretary/treasurer of the alumni society for the school. Ada also traveled with the family to Nova Scotia in 1894 to visit relatives.

Lizzie's husband, Patrick W. Ford, and his brother James E. Ford were both actively involved in the liquor trade in the 1890s and received multiple charges. The brothers were the sons of Thomas and Abbey Ford, Irish immigrants who originally settled in Boston before coming to Ellsworth, Maine. Thomas Ford was a disabled soldier from the Civil War, which put pressure on his seven children to become independent at a young age. Their older brother John was involved in buying liquor from a Boston liquor dealer before 1891. His mother, Abby Ford, endorsed a $100 promissory note for money that John owed liquor dealer H.W. Hughley & Company. In 1894, the jury decided in favor of the plaintiff, and Ford's mother had to pay the fee of $121.60 as damages. John wasn't involved in any other charges before his death in November 1897 of tuberculous (TB) at the age of thirty-one.

The Ford family had three saloon locations during the 1890s and early 1900s, two on West Street and one on lower Main Street. Besides the Fords, other West Street saloon owners who also had trouble with the police included the Herlihy brothers, John W. Guthrie, John McCarthy, Thomas T. Landers, Joshua Sweetsir, Thomas W. Underwood, Michael McCauley, J.J. McDonald, James Stewart, Hugh McKinley, Fred Johnson, R.A. Sproul, J.F. McFarland, William H. Foss, Benjamin and John A. Hatt, Edward Murray, Thomas H. Flanders and Patrick F. Bell.

After her husband's death, Lizzie Ford sold the saloon in the so-called Ford Building on Main Street in the autumn of 1902 to William Foss, and she moved to a new building next to J.J. Coney's Restaurant near the wharf. She continued to receive alcohol charges at the new location. Lizzie sold or closed her saloon business around 1905. There is not much news about her until she fractured both arms from a fall and was hospitalized in March 1906.

She recovered and married for the fourth time to Captain James L. Bray on November 5, 1908. Bray was her third sea captain husband and seemed to be the right match, which led Lizzie to finally retire from the liquor business. The couple lived at 6 West Street before moving to Livingston Road. Lizzie N. Bray did not outlive her fourth husband and died on February 8, 1919, at the age of sixty-nine of kidney disease.

Ada met Daniel H. Herlihy while visiting her mother. Herlihy was married to Cora Isabell "Belle" Higgins for a few years before she divorced him in October 1892 for adultery. Although Herlihy was a ladies' man with his Woodbine Club and other drinking establishments, Ada seems to have been the love of his life who tamed the man. By 1908, Ada was already assisting him with his Brewer Hotel business and other financial affairs. The couple married on June 15, 1914, and lived on Livingston Road next her sister Bethena and her husband, Ernest A. Graham, who lived in her mother's

A History Lover's Guide to Bar Harbor

West Street from the wharf showing saloons on the left of Lizzie Ford, John Coney and Dan Herlihy (Brewer Hotel) around 1900. *Courtesy of the Bar Harbor Historical Society.*

old house. Bethena was also very well educated and later was a member of the women's writing society the National League of American Pen Women.

After relocating to Bar Harbor and getting married, Ada continued working as an osteopathic physician from her home on Livingston Road. She kept her maiden name in all advertisements for her services in the *Bar Harbor Times* until she retired in 1919 at the age of forty-nine.

Dan Herlihy "welcomed" Prohibition and felt it provided a way to become "more powerful" and to make a "great amount of money."[21] After beginning operations in 1919, his "rum syndicate" served Maine and New England and was hugely successful until his indictment in 1923. Herlihy's illegal alcohol business made $200,000 to $300,000 a year ($3 million today) using a fleet of modern boats and trucks for acquisition and distribution. After raids by Howe Higgins in 1923—including 260 cases of whiskey seized in storage at John H. Stalford's Malvern Hotel greenhouses—George McKay, Arthur Falkenstrom, John H. Stalford and Daniel H. Herlihy were tried and convicted. In August 1923, Judge Peters of the U.S. District Court fined Stanley and Stalford $1,500 each; however, McKay got one year in Bangor jail and Herlihy was sentenced to one year in prison at the United States Prison in Atlanta, Georgia. This is the same George McKay who later owned the Criterion Theatre.

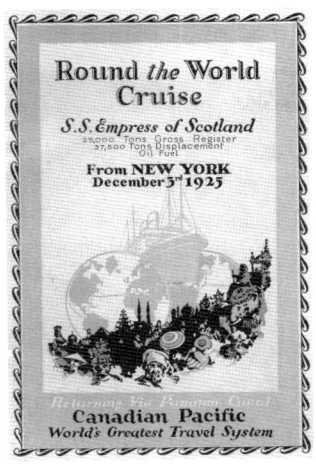

Brochure from Dan and Ada Herlihy's six-month cruise around the world in 1925–26 after his release from jail in Georgia for his bootlegging conviction. *Courtesy of the author.*

After serving his sentence, the first mention of Dan Herlihy's name in the newspapers, after a long absence, came in December 1925 when he and his wife left for their 120-day cruise around the world from December 1925 to April 1926. They left New York on the Canadian steamship *Empress of Scotland*, which went to Madeira; Gibraltar; Algiers; Nice; Monte Carlo; the Amalfi coast; Naples; Pompeii, the Holy Land, including Jerusalem, Nazareth (Christmas), Tiberius and Haifa; Egypt, including Cairo (New Year's), Giza (pyramids), Memphis, Luxor (Valley of the Kings and King Tut's tomb) and the Suez Canal; India, including Bombay, Madras, Deli, Agra (Taj Mahal), Calcutta and Ceylon; Asia, including Singapore, Hong Kong, the Great Wall of China, Japan and the Philippines; Hawaii; Los Angeles; San Francisco; the Panama Canal; Havana; and back to New York City.

Scott Fitzgerald said, "There are no second acts in American lives," but Dan Herlihy proved him wrong. When he returned to his Livingston Road residence, the Herlihys designed their dream club called Dreamwood. To avoid the issues of a Bar Harbor club, they chose Ireson Hill on a remote part of what today is known as Route 3. The property included an amazing dance floor and stage for top-tier bands to play and a sporting venue for boxing, wrestling and other competitions. The club opened on June 14, 1927, with two thousand patrons.

Dan and his wife received no alcohol violations during this post-incarceration period. To assume that no alcohol was ever present at Dreamwood or these boxing and wrestling matches is naive. A more likely situation was that Herlihy finally decided to act like many of the rich folks on the island and be less obvious about alcohol activities. He also was making a lot of money and likely diverted some of it to the right people to ensure he had no more problems with the Prohibition folks. Herlihy was no longer interested in running the alcohol distribution network. Instead, he let others do that while he profited from more legitimate businesses.

Dan Herlihy died after an illness of pneumonia that bothered his heart condition on July 29, 1932, during the peak of the season. His funeral was

Bar Harbor bootleggers returning from a Canada trip in the 1920s. *Courtesy of the author.*

in August, and many called at the big parlor at his house on Livingston Road "from all walks of life and of all ages each seeming to remember some kindness done them by Mr. Herlihy."[22] Stories of Herlihy as a quiet community benefactor to people and organizations added to his public image at his death.

The 1932 season continued with Ada doing her best to fill Dan's shoes. She managed the rest of the scheduled events for the summer, including the Labor Day Dance on September 5, 1932, and the Closing Ball and Farewell Benefit for Dick O'Day on Saturday, September 10, which had "souvenirs, prizes, and fortune for year 1933."[23] The season went well for boxing, with the Sawyer Twins making such a hit at the Dreamwood during the season that they gave a boxing exhibition in the fall. Although the house on Livingston Road was put up for sale, no one bought the house, and Ada continued to live there.

In April 1933, Ada was focused on keeping the Dreamwood open as a tribute to her late husband and called the club "D.H. Herlihy's Dreamwood," with an "atmosphere of a great home ballroom."[24] Ada hired a band to perform for the preseason Saturday night dances from 8:00 p.m. to 12:00 a.m. and the season Tuesday, Thursday and Saturday dances. Cecil Hutchinson and His Royal Commanders was the band in the early part of the season that later was replaced by Perley Reynold and His

Commanders. The admission price for the preseason dances was sixty-five cents for "gentlemen" and thirty-five cents for "ladies."

Ada used her travel experiences for the themes of her balls that summer. The Dreamwood went Spanish for its formal opening, which was called "A Night in Spain," with a masked Spanish orchestra playing music from 8:30 p.m. to 1:30 a.m. Her Chinese Ball was a "beautiful affair with a large crowd,"[25] with favors of Chinese umbrellas for the ladies and unusual Oriental oddities for the men. Ada wore a "valuable and extraordinarily beautiful wedding dress of the high caste Chinese woman" with a "16th century Mandarin coat of cloth of gold."[26] The August Cruise Around the World Ball provided a decorated Dreamwood with posters of different countries on the walls. Other balls included the April 29 opening with the Grand Prosperity Ball, Chauffeur's Charity Ball on August 22, Labor Day Ball with a New York Floor Show Revue and the Varsity Ball for the closing at the end of September. This was her last season running the club.

Ada Herlihy died on June 23, 1935, of pneumonia at her sister's house on Livingston Road next door to her house. She was said to have had "keen mentality, high intellectually, and was a wide reader."[27] She also had a "beauty of her character felt instantly by those that went into her presence."[28] The previous winter, she was "involved with writing historical subjects as she always had a facile pen."[29] Throughout her life, Dr. Herlihy was interested in English history and at an early age began to "collect with a discriminating eye a library of English history, literature biography and art."[30] "By the time of her death she had assembled some 3,000 volumes, many of them valuable rarities," which she donated to the Colby College Library in Waterville, Maine.[31] Her house was eventually purchased on May 15, 1936, by Dr. V.M. Manchester, who opened an office as an "Osteopathic physician and surgeon at the Daniel Herlihy House."[32]

On December 20, 1936, the Dreamwood, with its 84-by-137-foot ballroom and its 12-foot porches, was destroyed by fire. The *Bar Harbor Times* noted on December 25, 1936, that the Dreamwood opened on June 14, 1927, and its first big event was at the American Legion on July 5, 1927. The largest crowd was for Ted Lewis and his band, and other performers included Rudy Vallée (1934), Duke Ellington, Ozzie Nelson and Cab Calloway. The owners vowed to rebuild the venue, but it never reopened.

Franklin Delano Roosevelt was elected president in 1932, and Prohibition was repealed, but it took Bar Harbor a couple of years to catch up with the rest of the country. The "Original Malt Liquor applications" in June 1936 for Bar Harbor included Malvern Hotel, Earl Connors, Preston Joy, Michele

Testa (Main Street), Alma M. Bernadini (Main Street), Ezra Cough (Cottage Street), Curtis and Elizabeth Tracy, Pauline Higgins, Susan F. Lambert (Main and South Streets), Ida M. Redding, H.N. Silk (Cottage Street), J.W. Doyle (Jo's Sandwich Shop, Rodick Street), Millie Hunton, Bar Harbor Club, the Sunrise Hotel, Clarence L. Leonard (Cottage Street) and Betty Allison.[33] Three months later, Bar Harbor passed the referendum for liquor in September, and the town was "wet." At least six women applied for liquor licenses in 1936. If only Lizzie Ford and Ada Bearse lived to see the day.

Bonus Historical Sites: Many generations of visitors have enjoyed making a wish and throwing a coin in the Agamont Park Fountain, which was purchased from Swedish immigrant Eric E. Soderholtz in 1935. Soderholtz's garden pottery was a fixture in many Mount Desert Island cottages.

Although the original Testa's Restaurant building is gone, the iconic family-owned restaurant survives at 53 Main Street, where the business was established in 1934 by Michele Testa. He renovated the old Joy's restaurant that had been run by Preston Joy for thirty-six years and in 1941 bought the building between his restaurant and Millie's Restaurant and expanded the business by building a modern two-story, sixteen-room hotel and restaurant, replacing an undertaker and pool hall. Testa started his original restaurant in Palm Beach in 1921, and for nearly a century, the motto "Pines in the Summer, and Palms in the Winter" was used to illustrate their two seasonal businesses at opposite ends of the East Coast, Bar Harbor and Palm Beach. The old Bar Harbor building was replaced with a new building in 1990, and the Palm Beach location, which had occupied the same street corner for generations, closed in 2017.

In 1974, Gerry "Geddy" Mitchell transformed the bar at 19 Main Street into an entertainment mecca called Geddy's Pub with performances by Bonnie Raitt, Wynton Marsalis, Taj Mahal, Pure Prairie League, Arlo Guthrie, Livingston Taylor and Los Lobos. In 1987, the Davis family purchased Geddy's, and it became a popular family restaurant. The building was once owned by popular Italian businessman Tullio Bojer, who sold peanuts, cigars, candy, hot dogs and ice cream to visitors and locals for over forty years. He bought the business in the 1910s from Angelo Sinischalci, who came to Bar Harbor from Ecolano, Italy, in 1887. The Bar Harbor House hotel once stood on the site before it burned in 1918. Several of the other buildings on lower Main Street were built between 1880 and 1920, including the American Express Company Office/Millie's Restaurant/Tripp's Restaurant/Acadia Outdoors and Jordon Pond Ice Cream & Fudge

Shop (45 Main Street, 1911) and Green and Copp Company (successor to Green and Reynolds Company)/Jack's Jewelry (27 Main Street, 1887).

The property featured at the beginning of this chapter, Galyn's Restaurant, was a saloon built in 1892 and located between the Brewer Hotel (aka Cunningham Hotel) and the Bar Harbor House. The building has been a restaurant and hotel/rooming house over the years and may have been the first Lizzie Ford building; however, determining business locations is difficult since the Rodick Reality Company owned much of the land on lower Main Street into the 1920s.

The beautiful look of Main Street sidewalks that we see today was due to the work of Doug Chapman in the 1970s.

Chapter 3

THE RETURN OF EDEN'S PRODIGAL SONS: HERB REDDING AND SMYLIE GRANT ELLS

SHERMAN'S BOOK STORE
56 MAIN STREET

One of the things that has not been discussed enough was the effect decades of interaction with the summer residents had on the local population. Prior to the boom of the 1870s, families made their living primarily from the sea or logging. With the arrival of wealthy summer residents who required various services for their annual visits, the economy changed to incorporate this summer boom, and so did the local people.

The young people became much more worldly than their parents through their conversations and interactions with these rich visitors. They also developed different dreams and goals. Many wanted to find a way to join the group of rich people and emulate their lifestyle. Others followed the rich to their playground in Florida to continue their interaction. Two boys who grew up on opposite sides of Frenchman Bay embraced the lifestyle of the visitors and spent their lives connecting with the elite to better their own lives.

Herbert "Herb" Redding was born in 1883 and raised in Gouldsboro. His father was a house painter, and as a young man, Herb traveled across the bay with his father to work for the rich summer visitors. He soon realized that he was a natural businessman. Over the next six decades, Herb managed several successful businesses catering to the rich because he felt he knew what they wanted.

Ulysses Smylie Grant Ells (aka Smylie or S. Grant) was born in Eden (Bar Harbor) in 1885 and was the son of an economically troubled storekeeper

56 Main Street (stop no. 3), the former Keucher's Drug Store, which today is Sherman's Book Store. *Courtesy of the author.*

with serious health issues. Smylie worked as a newspaper distributor on the Steamship Wharf to make money for his family. It was on this wharf that he began to mimic the mannerisms of the rich. Smylie, with only a sixth-grade education, would soon be able to fool the savviest observer that he had a Harvard degree and was a blueblood. He also had a charismatic personality that motivated people to love him and believe him. He could have been a cult leader.

The two young men met in Bar Harbor either on the Steamship Wharf or possibly at one of the illegal saloons to begin their lifelong friendship. Herb was the more stable one of the pair. He grew up in a household with parents who were healthy and remained married for many years. Herb married in 1908 and remained married to his wife, Lena, for over fifty years. They had two children, Herbert Jr. and Gwendolyn. He owned houses and established several businesses with employees.

Smylie's story was a lot different due to two significant things that occurred in the first eighteen years of his life that influenced the remaining five decades he lived. First, he watched his family fall into poverty as the rich summer visitors enjoyed a comfortable lifestyle on the island. Besides working in his father's store, he sold newspapers to the rich people on the Steamship

Wharf. He saw how the rich moved and spoke and quickly mimicked them. This skill would prove extremely valuable to him and enable him to pursue his dreams of a better, more comfortable life.

The second factor was health related. Sometime during the first decade of the twentieth century, Smylie was infected with tuberculosis, the contagious bacterial infection. The disease destroyed one of his lungs in his youth and plagued him for the rest of his life. For over fifty years, he struggled with TB, and his ill health gave him a feeling that life was a joke. Before the 1950s, the disease usually became progressive and resulted in early death. The only treatment was to go to sanitariums where patients participated in a regimen of open air, ample meals and rest. Unlucky sanitarium guests left in a box by train at night. Smylie, fortunately, was always healthy enough to continue his adventures.

Smylie's brother Edward died of the disease in 1900 at the age of twenty-one after a troubled youth. Edward already had a record when he was caught in 1893 stealing "a lot of stuff" from his father's store, including thirty pounds of tea, fifty pounds of charcoal, twenty-five pounds of fish, ten pounds of pork, ten pounds of tomatoes and two gallons of rum. After two more larceny convictions, he was caught stealing a pair of trousers from James A. Robinson & Son's store on Main Street by the manager, Fountain Jellison. The *Bar Harbor Record* called Edward "Durance Vile," which means long prison sentence. This nickname would have been a fitting description of the ordeal that Smylie endured with TB.

In January 1904, Smylie's family sent him to a TB cure cottage in Saranac Lake, New York, where he nearly died not long after coming to the town. Although he told his nephew Jack Ells that he was shot in the back by a jealous gangster as he attempted to jump out of the bedroom window of his cure cottage, the real story was less glamourous. Smylie became depressed from his condition and shot himself in the stomach after drinking with friends. He was seriously injured in his abdomen and spine, and the newspaper accounts of the time called him the "Iron Man" because he survived the serious injury. He carried the slugs in his back for the rest of his life. One account had him drinking beer after one month of recovery. He never again felt sorry for himself and fought his illness with dignity for the rest of his life. In 1911, Smylie stayed in the Markleton Sanitarium, a private hotel/sanitarium in Pittsburgh, where he recovered from a serious operation that removed part of his lung damaged from the TB.

After his return to Bar Harbor, Smylie and Herb spent some time together before Smylie took off to New York City to seek his fortune mixing with the rich and powerful. He had already mastered his rich person impersonation and quickly became part of the New York scene, rubbing elbows with the Delmonico crowd at 2 South William Street in Lower Manhattan, including "Diamond Jim" Brady and Lillian Russell. Smylie was a popular cigarette salesman who gave away samples and sold cigarettes for M. Melachrino & Company Egyptian Cigarette Company and later Camp Importation Company of New York. Both companies provided initial, monogram and club handmade Turkish cigarettes. In 1915, he sold cigarettes from his brother's dental office in Bar Harbor for the summer season above Keucher's Drug Store/Sherman's Book Store (56 Main Street).

Herb continued to live in Bar Harbor during the 1910s but started to emulate the rich lifestyle by traveling in the off-season to Miami and West Palm Beach, Florida, where he began his real estate business. He also traveled with his family out west to California and Colorado, which was a change from his Gouldsboro lifestyle. Like many Maine families, Herb's parents and other family members eventually moved to the Boston area for better year-round work opportunities.

Eight months after the United States declared war on Germany in 1917, Smylie joined the U.S. Army at the age of thirty-two. Unfortunately, he was designated 4F due to serious health problems from TB (one lung) and other ailments (bullet in his spine, diabetes and underweight). The determined Smylie would not accept this rejection. Legend has it that he blackmailed an abortion doctor to provide documentation of his good health and supplied the enlisting officer with booze to accept the application. Thus, Smylie began his next adventure in the U.S. Army.

His military service included some of the best years of his life. After his enlistment in Miami on December 15, 1917, the first eight months of his service were at Fort Joseph E. Johnson in Jacksonville. Smylie used this opportunity to create a whole new image by using his experience in New York and pretending to be a New York City broker. A newspaper clipping from an unknown newspaper printed during the first few months of his service reveals how quickly he integrated himself into the group of prominent young businessmen from his division.

Smylie was promoted to second lieutenant of the Quartermaster Corps in August 1918 and sent to Portland, Oregon. He was then transferred to Eberts Field in Lenoke outside of Little Rock, Arkansas, with the Quartermaster Corps, Receiving Company No. 1. When Smylie left Portland, he had no money but soon won enough money playing cards with his fellow train passengers to enjoy his trip to Arkansas.

After arriving in Arkansas, he became close with the aviators at Eberts Field. The top ace and flight commander there was Thomas J. Lenihan from California. A photo sent to Herb Redding in March 1919 shows the two friends in their full army uniforms posing for the camera. Sadly, a few months later on July 12, Lenihan was killed in an air crash in his Curtiss plane while distributing flyers for a minstrel show in the fog. Smylie accompanied the body back to California.

When Smylie was discharged in August 1919, the "flying officer to a man expressed the keenest regret at the departure of Lieut. Ells," and I.S. Purdy, officer in charge of flying, said that "he has extraordinary wit and an ability to read those whom he comes in contact as if by an unerring intuition."[34] Purdy added, "These qualities tempered by the most human regard and consideration for others have gained for him a place in the heart of every man."[35] After returning to Bar Harbor after his discharge, Smylie went to Florida with Herb in the winter of 1919–20.

In the 1920s, Herb continued to spend more time in Miami and St. Augustine. A *Bar Harbor Times* newspaper report in 1925 by Gardner Maurice Sherman reported that during his visit to the town, Redding was busily at work behind a glass-topped desk in a fine office in the center of this historic old city.[36] Under the glass on his desk was a blueprint of Araquay Park, the large eight-hundred-acre subdivision of which he was part owner and secretary of the corporation. This was a boom time for Florida development, which eventually went bust in the late 1920s, a few years before the crash of 1929. During the summer, Herb was in Bar Harbor as a promoter of boxing matches at the Casino. In the 1930s, he moved to St. Petersburg, where he wintered for many years and often watched baseball spring training games.

In the 1920s, Smylie began his new role of gigolo. After his return from the Great War, Smylie married a rich widow, Elizabeth Braun Goldston, on May 26, 1921. Family stories have linked her to the Gillette fortune. From the existing records, Elizabeth (also known as Lil) was about seven years older than Smylie, and her parents were from Germany.

During the '20s, Smylie spent most of his time in Florida and New York City. He managed a real estate firm in Miami and judged a dance contest in St. Augustine in 1926 at the Ponce de León Hotel, which is now part of Flagler College. Jack Ells remembered him traveling with Lil to Bar Harbor and staying at the Columbia Cottage (the Field) one summer. In April 1926, Smylie traveled by ship to Merida, Mexico, to acquire a divorce from Lil after he used up most of her money. By June 1930, they were back living together in New York City. The reconciliation was due to Smylie's economic

Left: Smylie Grant Ells and Herb Redding in Florida in the 1920s. *Courtesy of the author.*

Right: Smylie Grant Ells in Merida, Mexico, getting a divorce in April 1926. *Courtesy of the author.*

problems and physical disability. She inherited more money, which he used up before jilting her again.

In the early 1930s, Smylie Ells and Herb Redding went to Bar Harbor and borrowed money from many of their old friends for one of their real estate ventures in Florida or New York. Herb had a great reputation in town as a trustworthy businessman specializing in boxing matches at the Casino and great fun at pool halls, speakeasies and gambling establishments. Something went wrong with this venture, and their fortunes took a dive due to the business slowdown of the Great Depression.

After this debacle, both Herb and Smylie felt compelled to stay away from Bar Harbor for seventeen years, not wishing to stir up any anger. This self-imposed exile was probably a bigger hardship to Herb since he had closer business ties to the town. For Smylie, the biggest problem was his relationship with his brother, who was a prominent civic leader. Herb's wife, Lena, came back to Bar Harbor in 1947 and stayed with her daughter at the Central House on Cottage Street. Then Herb and his son returned in 1948 to test

Herb Redding, his wife, his son and Smylie Grant Ells during their return to Bar Harbor in 1949. *Courtesy of the author.*

the water. Finally, Smylie joined him in October 1949 with Herb's wife and son for the funeral of Herb's half brother Arthur Hunton. At that time, Smylie went around and visited those people still alive who he owed money and offered to pay them back. His old friends were happy to see him and refused to accept a cent.

Smylie spent the later years of his life working for Herb in York, Maine, as the hotel manager of the Redding York Beach Hotel. Herb bought the hotel in 1941 from Arthur Libby. Photos survive of Smylie's happy days working in the resort town in southern Maine. He is pictured posing with celebrities and attractive young women on the beach and in front of the hotel. His ex-wife, Lil, traveled to York and worked in the gift shop of the Redding Hotel to be near him while he managed the hotel.

In the 1950s, Smylie's heath declined, and he ended up living at the Veterans Hospital in Rutland, Massachusetts, which specialized in veterans with TB. His nephew Jack Ells came to visit him often, and during one visit Smylie asked Jack to bring him a pair of his wife's underwear so that he could play a joke on the nurses. He later hid the item in the bed, and when the nurse spotted them, Smylie quickly grabbed them, attempting to hide his naughty deed. He had a sign outside his door that said "Captain Ells" even though his highest rank was second lieutenant. Smylie died at the hospital on March 14, 1955.

In the months leading up to his death, Smylie planned his funeral. He considered getting buried at Arlington Cemetery in Virginia due to his veteran status but instead opted for the First Parish Church in York, Maine, not far from the Redding Hotel. Herb Redding bought the plot that is marked with a "Veterans" marker. Smylie had a U.S. Marine regiment at his funeral and a bugle player played Taps, which did not leave a dry eye in the place. After the burial, the attendees went to the Redding Hotel for a reception in his honor. At the reception, a letter written by Smylie was read. In the letter, he stated that he had "no regrets and had lived a useful life." At the end of the note, he remarked that maybe he did have one regret. After a pause, the reader indicated that Smylie regretted not giving the burial business to a friend, O'Grady (O'Grady's Funeral Home). The whole crowd laughed. Smylie entertained to the very end. Ten years later, Smylie's dear fried Herb Redding died on February 25, 1965, at the age of eighty in York.

Lost Main Street: John W. Doe/Gonya Drug Store (67 Main Street) and Green Brothers Store/GAR Hall (57 Main Street) buildings on either side of the corner of Main and Cottage Streets.

Chapter 4
BAR HARBOR VILLAGE IMPROVEMENT ASSOCIATION AND THE ONE-HORSE TOWN

MORRISON BUILDING
62 MAIN STREET

The Bar Harbor Village Improvement Association (BHVIA), founded in 1881, had an early membership that read like a who's who in America, with prominent members such as John S. Kennedy, Mrs. Joseph Pulitzer, Mrs. J.P. Morgan, Mrs. George Vanderbilt, Ernesto Fabbri, Dr. Augustus Thorndike, Alfred du Pont and Dr. Robert Abbe. With the aid of Waldron Bates, George Dorr and Beatrix Ferrand, the BHVIA was "instrumental in designing Bar Harbor's downtown, parks and gardens, as well as Kebo Valley Club House, one of the oldest nine-hole golf courses in the US in the 1890s (later expanded to 18 holes in 1920), and the boundaries and trails of Acadia National Park."[37]

The BHVIA "had an immediate and lasting impact on the community and its residents" through actions promoting the "health, welfare and beautification" of the area, as well as "economic and operational initiatives."[38] Although the organization had several prominent summer residents as members, many of the members of the BHVIA were local residents who "played a major role in shaping policies, implementing them and providing skilled local labor to perform the work."[39] Although the BHVIA did not have the legal power to enforce actions, the members from the summer colony were able to pressure the town government to cooperate with their proposed changes. Their health-oriented achievements included "a sewer system, garbage incineration, regulation of stables, and inspection of water and milk supplies."[40] One example is the BHVIA hiring the local firm the

62 Main Street (stop no. 4), the 1897 Morrison Building, which was the telephone exchange for many years. *Courtesy of the author.*

Shea brothers to cut two seats for the Village Green from pink granite that were five feet long, twenty-three inches high and twenty-three inches deep in October 1905.

One of the critical problems for the town, prior to the arrival of cars on the island in 1913, was the removal of horse manure from the streets each evening after midnight. The responsibility for cleaning the roads went to the Roads and Paths Committee of the BHVIA, chaired by George B. Dorr. The Sanitary Committee may also have played a part in the cleanup since it helped with the establishment of a Board of Health and a health officer to enforce sanitary regulations. The main resource was personnel to perform the cleanup, which was critical during the summer months.

As a college student at the University of Pennsylvania around 1910, John B. Ells needed a summer job to earn money for his expenses and took a job as member of the BHVIA shoveling the horse excrement out of the streets after midnight each evening. On one summer night, two men walked into town from the wharf addressing an urgent matter. Apparently, the cook on the summer resident's yacht had died, and the men wanted to call the man's family to notify them. Telephone service increased in Bar Harbor between 1879 and the early 1900s since the number of cottages in Bar

Harbor went from fourteen to several hundred.[41] Although Bar Harbor had at least six hundred phones installed in town at that time and twelve switchboard operators at the local exchange, everything in Bar Harbor was closed at that hour.

After a visual search of the town, the two men walked up to John Ells and the other BHVIA workers and asked if they knew where they could find a telephone to place this emergency call. John told them that the Newport House had a telephone but was closed. He also added that the Western Union office had a phone, but that, too, was closed, and the man who ran it had a gun and did not want to be disturbed after he went to bed. Then one of the men spotted the telephone exchange office on Main Street and asked if there were any telephones available in that office. John informed the man that the female operators carried on so bad with their boyfriends in the building that their manager locked the door when he left and prohibited the girls from opening the door for any reason. The two men were now very disgusted with the town, and one of the men said, "If you ask me, this place is nothing more than a one-horse town." John responded saying, "Mister, if you had my job you would not call this a one-horse town."

Mosaic tile floor in the entrance to the former Bar Harbor telephone exchange at 62 Main Street. *Courtesy of Richard Duperey.*

The original telephone exchange was established by George H. Grant in the Grant Building/Christmas Shop (80 Main Street, 1897) and later moved to the Morrison Building/Stadium Restaurant (62 Main Street, 1897), where the word "TELEPHONE" in mosaic can still be found on the entrance floor. This building was originally built by Mark C. Morrison as the Marlborough Pharmacy after he moved from the Rogers Pharmacy/Village Pharmacy (Rogers Block, 1887) near Albert Meadow.

Other Main Street Sites: Emery Block Building/Sunset Hotel/Bar Harbor Savings & Loan (103 Main Street, 1900); West End Drug (105 Main Street, 1900) with Gilfillan family ownership (1918–2018); Lyford Woodward Building/Fenton et. al. Law Offices (109 Main Street, 1887); Caleb's/The Barnacle (112 Main Street, 1900); F.H. Moses Florist Shop/Stone Soup (113 Main Street, 1904); Mary Jane/Carmen Verandah/Bar Harbor Beer Works (119 Main Street, 1887); Sproul's Café/Ward Building (128 Main Street, 1880); Pine and Palm Florist/Acadia Corporation (134 Main Street, 1883); Butterfields/Sailor & Hook (154 Main Street, 1887); and Bar Harbor Electric Light Company/Bangor Hydro Building (18 Edgewood Street, 1892).

Chapter 5

THE BRADLEY BLOCK

FIRST NATIONAL BANK
102 MAIN STREET

For those who visited or lived in Bar Harbor in the last fifty years, the parking lot between the Bar Harbor Trust Company and the First National Bank building on Main Street has been a familiar sight. For those people who grew up prior to the 1960s, they remember the massive building called the Bradley Block that filled that space. This ghost building is always present when reviewing old pictures of Main Street, along with the other massive ghost building, the Rodick House, which was located across the street.

The beginning of the story of the Bradley Block started with the purchase of the land by Bryant Bradley from Stephen Higgins on September 24, 1874. Some accounts have him building a four-story building in 1874, and most say the building was completed in 1879. Bradley considered the building an investment property that hosted his studio and provided space for other business tenants to serve the guests of the massive Rodick House across the street. Much of the advertisements in the paper during this early era stressed the proximity to this hotel. By the early 1880s, the Bradley Block gained fame and was featured in the bird's-eye view map of Bar Harbor on the same level as other major landmarks in the town such as the Hotel Des Isles (1881), Grand Central Hotel (1873), Episcopal church (1878), Rodick House (1866–82) and the West End Hotel (1879).

Bradley, a photographer who sold scenes of Mount Desert Island to tourists and rich summer visitors, advertised services that included "a large selection of stereoscopic and large views of Mount Desert scenery for sale.

A History Lover's Guide to Bar Harbor

102 Main Street (stop no. 5), the First National Bank building, erected in 1909, is next to the parking lot where the Bradley Block was located. *Courtesy of the author.*

Residences, Groups, Boating Parties, etc., photographed at short notice."[42] He sold his business to Ernest Emery in the late 1880s and worked as the store manager until a legal dispute caused him to establish a rival shop with his son. Bradley also focused his attention on civic and real estate activities. He died in 1899, and his son, Harry, carried on the photography business on Cottage Street until his death in June 1940.

Any discussion of the Bradley Block must begin with the definition of *block* in Bar Harbor. Early maps and real estate transactions designate sizable areas of private property ownership in town as "blocks." Bar Harbor blocks named for owners included Allen, Ash, Bradley, Brewer, Brick, Bunker, Cough, Cunningham, Dunbar, Ells, Emery, Fifield and Haynes, Foster, Grant, Hamor, Higgins, Jellison & Whitney, Morrison, Mount Desert, Pineo, Porcupine, Povich, Roberts, Rodick and Rogers. There was a Freeman Block in Southwest Harbor and a Berry Block in Rockland that were also mentioned frequently in the old Bar Harbor newspapers.

The Bradley Block building had four stores on the street level. Early tenants included Frank Moore, dealer in watches, clocks and jewelry, spectacles and eye glasses, silver and plated ware; SD Wiggins and Company, druggists and apothecaries maker of Wiggins' Cherry Cordial for coughs, colds, hoarseness and sore throats; Irving H. Davis, owner of "the fashionable, cool tonsorial parlor" (barbershop); Chas. C. Burrill, banker, insurance and ticket agent; Dr. Rogers; and L.S. Chilcott, DDS, graduate of the Philadelphia Dental College, who may have been one of the local dentists that provided a model for John B. Ells's career.

Dr. Charles C. Morrison (aka old Dr. Morrison) moved his medical practice and residence to the block around 1883. His son, Dr. Charles C. Morrison Jr. (aka young Dr. Morrison), and his daughter, Mildred, were born there. He eventually purchased a third of the building that served as residence and office space for him and his brother, Elmer J. "E.J." Morrison, who had a dental office. E.J. Morrison later became a medical doctor in Bar Harbor and was the medical examiner for Hancock County for many years. In 1908, Everett J. Hinckley, DDS, moved into the Morrison dental office.

Dr. Charles Morrison Sr., a prominent resident whose first office was in the Bradley Block. *Courtesy of Lorena Caler.*

The Bar Harbor Masons (Bar Harbor Lodge No. 185, F. & A.M.) used space in one of the upper floors during the 1880s on the third Thursday of each month. W.F. Holland, A.L. Higgins and Bryant Bradley were active as officers in the rites performed in the building.

Moore's Jewelry Store was the first jewelry store established in the block. Later, Sawyer Jewelry Store took over the space for about seventy years until 1955, when it moved across the street to the Harmon building, formerly the Clement's Music Store.

Lufkin's of Bangor operated a candy store in another one of the building stores for forty-six years, managed by Grace Lufkin. Lufkin worked at the store until she retired at the age of eighty-seven. The business was purchased by Eileen Burnett in 1950.

Adeline Higgins entered a lease in April 1897 to "rent rooms and give table board to her lodgers" for the summer while her house (227 Main Street) was rented out to Gardiner Sherman, member of the New York Stock Exchange. She continued the Bradley Block boardinghouse for thirty-five years until her death in 1934.

In December 1922, a devastating fire raged in the venerable building. Most of the inventory of the stores on the first level was able to be removed

Bradley Block photographed by Bryant Bradley in 1881 showing the Rodick House across the street and signs for the Berry Bros. Stable and the John Dean Café. *Courtesy of Southwest Harbor Library.*

from the site before the fire, smoke and water damaged the building. The upper floor was damaged badly and never replaced. So much water was poured on the fire that the building was covered with frozen ice after the fire was extinguished.

The building was repaired by E.C. Webb and his crew of men, including a new roof. The previous first-floor tenants returned for the 1923 season, including Sawyer Jewelry Store, Lufkin's Candy Shop, the Toy Shop (Mrs. Hinch's) and L.M. Hamilton & Company women's shop. Mrs. Higgins's rooming house returned with fewer rooms for rent.

After the fire, Tobias Roberts bought Dr. Morrison's portion of the building. His uncle W.M. Roberts had control of the other two-thirds until his death in February 1929, when much of the building was put in a trust managed by Tobias Roberts and Mary R. Sprague to generate income for his widow. When Mrs. Roberts died in 1934, the ownership went to her niece and nephew. On Wednesday, February 27, 1929, fire again came close but missed burning the block.

For many years, Mrs. Frank Foster had a toy shop in one of the building's stores. In later years, Mrs. Margaret White operated a yarn shop, which was formerly a dry goods store owned by Mark Perlinsky. During the summers, linen stores occupied the store. Miss Florence Lewis operated a dry goods business in Mrs. Foster's old store after she left. In 1957, the First National Bank of Bar Harbor and Mount Desert Block Company bought the Bradley Block. It was later demolished to build the parking lot.

First National Bank (102 Main Street), designed by Andrews, Jaques and Rantoul, appeared in all photos of the Bradley Block after it was built in 1909.

Bonus Historical Site: The Bar Harbor Bank & Trust (82 Main Street) in the Mount Desert Block (1886) was where Sheldon Goldthwait, bank president, experienced some of Dr. John B. Ells's self-deprecating humor in 1948, the day after the defeat of Thomas Dewey to Harry S. Truman in the U.S. presidential election. The Bar Harbor GOP and the bank were active campaigners for Dewey, and his surprise loss was a huge defeat. The day after the election was rainy, and Sheldon received a call from Dr. Ells around noon. All Ells said was, "Look out the back window of the bank. Dewey is all wet." When Sheldon looked out the window, he saw a large campaign banner used during the campaign hanging from two trees behind the bank near the now lost Ocean House (1870). All the ink from the banner was running out of the picture of Dewey's face in the rain. Ells and Sheldon laughed for several minutes and healed their disappointment from the loss.

Chapter 6
BEE'S STORE AND MISS SHAW

BAR HARBOR HEMPORIUM
116 MAIN STREET

Bee's Store was established by Albert W. Bee on Main Street during the 1870s. Mr. Bee was called the "locally famous and indispensable provider of summer literature" and "caramels, cigarettes, and chewing-gum," and his store was located across the street from the Rodick House.[43] The newspaper advertisements for the store in the 1880s provided an inventory that included New York, Boston, Philadelphia and Bangor newspapers; all types of stationery and writing materials; and candy for summer residents. Bee was known for delivering the newspapers to customers at the earliest possible moment and chartered steamship excursion trips on the steamer *Mount Desert* to pick up the *Sunday Herald* newspapers on the mainland. Bee was called the "original summer business man of Bar Harbor, and one of the most successful," with "the highest personal and business character, and a man of excellent, important, and comprehensive mental grasp of public affairs."[44] He moved his store in the 1880s to 116 Main Street (1880). In 1895, he tried to resurrect the Rodick House by leasing the old hotel after it was closed for two years in an unsuccessful attempt to reestablish its past glory. The old hotel closed permanently in 1906 and was torn down.

The Bees were from the Boston area, where they wintered every year and maintained two stores. One was on Tremont Street in Boston and the other in the Boston suburbs. During the summers, they stayed at their cottage in Southwest Harbor called Sleepy Hollow.

In the 1880s or 1890s, Bee hired a young woman named Isa Dora Shaw from Warren County, Massachusetts. She was the daughter of Thomas and

A History Lover's Guide to Bar Harbor

116 Main Street (stop no. 6), former location of Bee's Store and today the Bar Harbor Hemporium. *Courtesy of the author.*

Nancy Shaw and was born in 1860. Miss Shaw later became his "assistant in management" and most important employee.

Shaw never married or had her own children; however, she had a big influence on the lives of three men from three different generations whom she treated as sons: Harold O. Rodick, John B. Ells and Newall Rumery. Although little is known about her relationship with Rodick and Rumery, the story of her importance in the life of John B. Ells was passed down to his family.

In the late 1890s, Shaw hired John B. Ells to work at the store. His brother Smylie's work selling newspapers at the Steamship Wharf may have introduced the young man to Mr. Bee. John's family life was stressful as his mother struggled with the deaths of her eldest son and her husband; the loss of her daughter to adoption by a relative; and homelessness. She did not provide much parental guidance to her youngest son, and he came to work with a dirty face and hands. Shaw cleaned him up and became a surrogate parent for the boy. She saw something in him that others dismissed due to his family's issues. With her encouragement, John excelled in school, and she also supported his interest in civic activity in the town.

Miss Isa Dora Shaw at her house on Hancock Street, 1930s. *Courtesy of the author.*

Bee's Store on Main Street in the late 1800s. *Courtesy of the author.*

Ells later remembered her fondly and knew that she played a big part in his rising out of poverty to graduate from the University of Pennsylvania with a dental degree in 1913. Shaw and Bee's Store had an exclusive deal to sell newspapers to navy ships, which gave young Ells the opportunity to be the face of Bar Harbor for many officers and mariners. These contacts became valuable when, after being told that the University of Pennsylvania Dental School was full, an exception was made by one of the school officials who recognized him from his days selling newspapers on the wharf.

Bee, who was born in California, moved to Cupertino after 1902 and then to Burlingame near Santa Barbara in 1915. This was around the time that he sold the business to Shaw after running the store for forty years. She ran the store by herself for ten years and then sold it to Emma Clough in the mid-1920s. Albert Bee died in 1925 and his wife in 1939.

Miss Shaw lived in her house on Hancock Street for the remaining twenty years of her life. After John Ells's mother died in 1928, he looked after Shaw like she was his mother until she died in 1943 at the age of eighty-three. Since she had no heirs, Harold O. Rodick, John B. Ells and Newall Rumery were each given a one-third share of her estate in her January 21, 1944 probated will. The eldest of the three, John B. Ells, was appointed representative for her estate and received her house at 50 Hancock Street. As he did with his mother's house, which he inherited in 1928, Ells sold Shaw's house and remained living in his three-bedroom apartment over the *Bar Harbor Times* at 68½ Main Street near his beloved wharf.

Bonus Historical Site: Bar Harbor Town Clock (aka Village Clock) was presented to the town for Eden's centennial celebration in July 1896 by the BHVIA and was first located on the street in front of Albert Bee's Store (116 Main Street). The clock was later moved to its current location by the Village Green in 1905.

Chapter 7
THE WILL OF WILLIAM M. ROBERTS

ROBERTS MONUMENT
BAR HARBOR VILLAGE GREEN

When William Martin Roberts died on February 14, 1929, the town of Bar Harbor lost one of the most successful businessmen in its history. What made Roberts unique was how every aspect of his life was linked to the town and how he took an active part in the "development of the small village to a summer resort of nation-wide fame," including selling "a number of large and scenically important tracts," which are today part of Acadia National Park.[45] Although he made a sizable fortune during his lifetime, he was a dedicated native son who could mix with the summer residents but was most comfortable with people from the small town.

His father, Tobias L. Roberts, moved from Boston with his wife, Mary, in 1836 and opened a store for local fishmen and coasters. He was a key force in starting the tourist industry in the town by building the first summer hotel, the Agamont House, in 1855, along with a small wharf that provided a new entry to the town of Eden (Bar Harbor). His rustic hotel with cornhusk-stuffed mattresses helped replace the fading shipbuilding and fishing industries. The Agamont House was located on lower Main Street between today's Paddy's Restaurant/West Street Hotel and Testa's Restaurant.

After being educated in the local schools, William joined the family business in 1868 at the age of twenty. On Thanksgiving Eve 1869, he married twenty-year-old Mariam Ash from another local prominent family. Their only son, John Whittington Roberts, was born on August 22, 1870. Around this same time, his father, Tobias L. Roberts, established the first

A History Lover's Guide to Bar Harbor

John W. Roberts Monument (stop no. 7) in the Bar Harbor Village Green near the intersection of Main Street and Mount Desert Street. *Courtesy of the author.*

telegraph line connecting Eden (Bar Harbor) to the outside world via the Southwest Harbor/Ellsworth branch.

After expanding his own hotel, Tobias Sr. helped launch the career of two of his sons, Tobias Jr. and William, in the hotel business with the Rockaway House (1873) (site of Agamont Park today) and the Newport House (1869) (area south of Agamont Park between Bar Harbor Inn and Main Street), respectively. The Rockaway House and Newport House were the "first of the hotels to greet the eye of the summer visitors" and had the best view of the Porcupine Islands and Frenchman Bay of the early hotels in the town. Historian Cleveland Amory described the Newport House as "a place where one could walk and talk, and many congregated in front on piazzas, benches, and chairs around the lawn of this Bar Harbor resort making plans for their next adventure."[46] President Theodore Roosevelt's niece danced at a party at the Newport House in September 1906.[47]

Much can be learned about a person from their will, and W.M. Roberts's will was a very revealing document. Most of his estate went to the partner of his life of fifty-nine years, his wife, Mariam, who he left $40,000 and the interest from his investments. She continued to live at the Cadillac Cottage on Main Street per the agreement made with the Maine Central Railroad Company.

Although Roberts was very active with the horse industry in Bar Harbor—buying and selling horses, building the track at Morrell Park and participating in the Bar Harbor Horse Show—he is best known as an early auto enthusiast and big player in the campaign for legislation that admitted automobiles to the island in 1913. He built his own road for his cars to ride on from Eagle Lake to Bubble Pond in 1908. The will instructed the executers that "all motor cars are to be sold outside of Bar Harbor,"[48] which provided the best price to increase the value of the estate.

He also donated $400 in trust to maintain the Roberts Plot in the cemetery and the Bench on the Village Green in memory of his son. He chose to be buried in Old Village Cemetery (Mount Desert Street Cemetery) rather than to be interred in the more spacious, beautiful Ledgelawn Cemetery. This was a dedication to the town and his church, Bar Harbor Congregational Church, as well as his wife's church, St. Saviour's Episcopal Church. Of course, the monuments he built were the most elegant and durable stones in the cemetery besides the Civil War Monument. He also donated $500 to the Bar Harbor Congregational Church.

The John Whittington Roberts Bench (Roberts Monument) in the Village Green is one of the best memorials built in Bar Harbor. Countless citizens of the town, tourists and teenagers have used this bench over the years, which is a tribute to the son who died young of kidney disease in 1904. Although William M. Roberts lived a lavish life with five servants in his home, his son's death was a catastrophe for the Roberts family since he was the only one in the family who possessed the skills or ambition to carry on the business. The bench was installed in 1907.

Roberts worked through his grief with the purchase of the Marlborough Hotel (1882) in 1905 from Herbert Higgins as an annex to the Newport House. He later sold the entire hotel complex to the Maine Central Railroad in 1911 with the stipulation that he and his family could remain in the Cadillac Cottage until their deaths. His son's widow, Hannah Etta Roberts (Foster), lived with the Robertses until she remarried and established her own home in the 1920s.

William M. Roberts was very dedicated to the fire companies of the town. As an owner of several wood structures, he was committed to helping the town respond to fire emergencies. In his lifetime, he witnessed the destruction of the St. Sauveur Hotel (1870) owned by his sister and her husband, Fred Alley, in 1881 and his father's hotel, the Agamont House, in 1888. He gave $500 in his will to both the W.M. Roberts Hook and Ladder Company and the Bar Harbor Hose Company. Besides helping to erect a firehouse and buying horses, carriages and equipment, he also donated a phonograph from J.H. Sawyer's with twelve records to the club in 1904 for the firefighters to listen to during their downtime in their clubroom.

Roberts owned part of the famous Bradley Block in Bar Harbor on Main Street, which today is the parking area between two Bar Harbor banks. He gave portions of this property to his niece Mary R. Sprague and nephew Tobias L. Roberts to provide income for his widow during her remaining years.

William Martin Roberts's wife, Mariam, lived five more years, passing in February 1934. Besides giving personal items and cash to various family members, she gave the bulk of the remaining Roberts estate to her nephew Tobias L. Roberts and a trust to her niece Jane Parker. The Maine Central Railroad Company tore down the Newport House and other Roberts buildings in 1938. The Cadillac Cottage survived as the Harborview Hotel and Green Door bar before being razed in the late 1960s. The "steps to nowhere" in front of the Bar Harbor Inn sign is all that remains of the building.

When the Newport House closed in the 1930s, families in Bar Harbor bought the beds and used them for many years after. Connie Ells (Armstrong) was one of the people who slept many nights on a Newport House bed as a girl. One can only wonder if her bed was slept on by one of the famous visitors to the island during those glory years for the hotel. It is likely that the

William Martin Roberts's Newport House and Cadillac Cottage (later the Harborview Hotel). *Courtesy of the Bar Harbor Historical Society.*

William Martin Roberts's son John Roberts (*third from left*) with other bird hunters. *Courtesy of the Bar Harbor Historical Society.*

more than one thousand beds that came out of the Rodick House, Grand Central, West End Hotel and other Victorian-era hotels ended up part of Maine households in the twentieth century. Sadly, the beds of the Malvern (1882), Belmont (1879), DeGregoire hotels and the sixty-seven cottages that burned in the Fire of 1947 never had a chance for a second life.

Bonus Historical Site: The Bar Harbor Fire Department (37 Firefly Lane, 1911). Fountain Rodick Engine Company #1 (aka Mount Desert Hose Company) built the original building in 1882. In 1891, W.M. Roberts Hook and Ladder Company was established and later became part of the fire department with the Mount Desert Hose Company. The Acadia Information Center (19 Firefly Lane, 1927) (former Comfort Station) was built by A.B. and J.R. Hodgkins.

Chapter 8

THE CAR AND THE VILLAGE GREEN

VILLAGE GREEN BANDSTAND
VILLAGE GREEN, MAIN AND MOUNT DESERT STREETS

After years of growth following Roosevelt's election in 1932, the U.S. economy experienced a downturn in 1937–38. The Republicans said that the New Deal programs were unfriendly to business, and the Democrats said it was big business greed that slowed growth. Whatever the cause, Bar Harbor suffered economically from the downturn. The story of the 1939 car contest is interesting since Roosevelt's target for greed was Henry Ford and the key element of this story was a 1938 Ford Tudor sedan.

The Bar Harbor Village Green was originally the site of the 350-room Grand Central Hotel before the town bought and demolished the hotel in 1899. A few years later, it replaced the hotel with the park. The BHVIA worked with noted landscape architect Beatrix Farrand to redesign the park in the 1920s, moving the bandstand to its current location. It was in the bandstand in the Village Green in July 1939 that the winning ticket for the car contest was selected.

One-dollar raffle tickets went on sale in the town for the item in the Great Depression that many Americans could not afford to buy or even maintain—a car. The drawing of the ticket to benefit the Mount Desert Hospital was scheduled to take place on July 4, 1939. Dr. Ells, head of the Bar Harbor Republican Party, was to share the podium in the Village Green with John Ash, who was the master of ceremonies and organizer for most town events. Ells invited Owen Brewster, the leading U.S. House of Representatives member (former governor and future U.S. senator) from Maine, to make a speech and pick the winning number for the car. Dr.

Bar Harbor Village Green Bandstand (stop no. 8), where the 1939 drawing for the car occurred. *Courtesy of the author.*

Ells had known Brewster since the February 1926 Maine to the Southland Pilgrimage, where they met future president Herbert Hoover and President Calvin Coolidge in Washington, D.C., and Ells changed his party affiliation to Republican. Ells was running for reelection for board of selectmen for Bar Harbor and saw Brewster's visit as a boost to his election prospects. Brewster accepted the invitation after Dr. Ells guaranteed that no senior member of the Republican Party or their families would buy a ticket. Brewster was also running for reelection in 1940 and did not want anything embarrassing to happen during the campaign.

Dr. Ells told his wife, Charlotte "Lottie," not to buy a ticket and instead made a private donation to the hospital. His daughter Connie was twelve years old and wanted to win the car. Connie's grandmother Abigail Patriquin Brewer, the wife of Frank Brewer, who owned the Brewer Ice Company, did not know of Dr. Ells's ban on family ticket purchases. She was supportive of charities and saw the sign in the window of a store on Cottage Street concerning the hospital raffle. Although she had no interest in owning a car and did not even have a license, she bought a ticket at the Brown's Studio (6 Cottage Street, 1887) and had Connie sign her name on the ticket. Connie took the ticket, and all forgot about the ticket except Connie.

Above: Abbie Brewer, who bought the ticket for Connie Ells, with husband Frank Brewer, owner of the Brewer Ice Company, 1930s. *Courtesy of the author.*

Left: Constance Ells, winner of the car on July 4, 1939, with Sylvia Young. *Courtesy of the author.*

On the Fourth of July after Brewster's speech, Dr. Ells and John Ash prepared for the big drawing. In 1939, people were bad off, and the whole town came out for the drawing, hoping, as they held their tickets firmly in their hands, that they would be the winner. Connie, too, held her ticket firmly as she played with Sylvia Young and her friends on the steps of the bandstand in the Village Green waiting for the big drawing. She was now convinced more than ever that she possessed the winning ticket and informed her friends that she would win. As Brewster reached into the box and pulled out the winning ticket, the crowd was silent. Brewster handed the ticket to John Ash, who looked at the ticket and said, "Oh my God. Is my face red." Everyone in the crowd thought that Ash's wife, Shirley, won the car. He showed the ticket to Dr. Ells, and his face turned white. It was Connie's name on the ticket, and they had to announce the winner because everyone saw Brewster draw it. John Ash looked at the crowd and announced, "The winner is Connie Ells." Dr. Ells's face was still white as Connie entered the bandstand and accepted her prize. She could not understand why her father, John Ash and Brewster were not overwhelmed with happiness for her. As quickly as possible, Brewster, Dr. Ells and John Ash concluded the ceremony and disappeared.

John Ash, master of ceremonies at most Bar Harbor events in the 1930s and 1940s, at his desk. *Courtesy of the author.*

The July 1939 winning ticket for the 1938 Ford Tudor sedan. *Courtesy of the author.*

Later that night, after this grand embarrassment, Brewster consulted with Dr. Ells and pondered whether his political career was over. He needed Hancock County to win reelection in 1940 and felt Mount Desert Island would never vote for him after this fiasco. John suggested that the test would be his own selectman election in three months. If he won the election, Brewster would be fine. Apparently, the voters of Hancock County did not believe anyone would have been crazy enough to fix the drawing for the car, and both Dr. Ells and Brewster were reelected.

The only mention of the incident in the *Bar Harbor Times* was on page four of the July 6, 1939 edition after a recap of the July 4 events and prizes. The short news item said, "Miss Constance Ells, daughter of Dr. and Mrs. John B. Ells, won the Ford car which was given away."[49] Knowing her father's influence in town, the newspaper editor was most likely promptly contacted and told to bury the story. If anyone else won the car, the story would have been on the front page with a picture.

The car, a 1938 Ford Tudor sedan, was valued at $700 in 1939, but few had the money to buy it. Dr. Ells wanted to sell the car and use the money for Connie's college education. He did not want to deal with any financing for the car, so he sold it to a lobster fisherman who had a good catch and paid $400 cash for the car. Ten years later, Dr. Ells ran into the man he sold the car to on the wharf in Bar Harbor. The man informed Dr. Ells that he had just sold the car, which he used to transport fish for ten years, for $400. All Bar Harbor stories somehow end with the ocean.

Connie eventually used the $400 for college expenses at Syracuse University, where she met her husband, Quentin Armstrong. Her grandmother must have known the ticket would bring Connie good fortune for doing a charitable act.

Upper Main Street Sites (not on the trail): Adler's Town and Country Shop/Katahdin Photo Gallery (164 Main Street, 1925); Alton Jewett Store/Window Panes (166 Main Street, 1900); Old Lynam Building/Ivy Manor (194 Main Street, 1900); McKays Cottage (231 Main Street, 1897–99); Edgar Morang Residence/Tea House (278 Main Street, 1924); E.G. Jordan Building/Acadia Frameworks (288 Main Street, 1887); Bar Harbor Water Company/Anchorspace (337 Main Street, 1895); Breakwater (45 Hancock Street, 1903–04); Bide-A-While (6 Barberry Lane, 1896); Redwood (10 Barberry Lane, 1879); and Kenarden Gate Houses & Gates (352 Main Street, 1892).

Bonus Historical Site (not on the trail): As a boy, John B. Ells brought coal and wood to his aunt Adeline Higgins's house (227 Main Street, 1880), today the Lyman Insurance Company. Like a servant, he ate the scraps of meat in the kitchen while his sister Mabel feasted on choice pieces of meat in the dining room in her fine dresses. She treated him like a poor relation and would not acknowledge that they were siblings. At Christmas, Ells was given a small used toy by the family while Mabel had her own room full of new toys. He later became chairman of the group that provided needy children with new toys every Christmas.

Chapter 9

THE COASTER'S CHECKBOOK / ASH GRAVES

MOUNT DESERT STREET CEMETERY
41 MOUNT DESERT STREET

In 2002, Linda Carter Burroughs inherited 22 Ash Place after the death of her father, Harlan Carter. Her mother inherited the property from her relative Shirley Johnson Ash, the widow of John Ash, in 1978. Although she loved the house, Linda decided to sell it a year later. While she was cleaning out the third floor, she found items that belonged to the Ash family, including 180 pieces of paper that dated from 1842 to 1885. She quickly contacted Debbie Dyer and donated the collection to the Bar Harbor Historical Society. Debbie realized that they were the receipts of Captain Benjamin Ash, a Bar Harbor mariner in the 1800s who was John Ash's grandfather. Most of the receipts were for purchases and debts connected to Captain Ash and his widow, Maria (aka Mariah) Higgins Ash. The collection ended in 1885 when Mrs. Ash came under the care of her daughter Almira Ash.

The receipts provide a window into the nineteenth century, showing the various products and services purchased, the cost of items and the vendors providing services. Only a few receipts reveal information about money that Captain Ash received for his coasting services between Bar Harbor and Rockland. These financial transactions should not be viewed as a complete inventory of his purchases during this period since not all personal and business transactions involved receipts in the 1800s and many purchases may have been conducted with cash or barter. Due to the scarcity of paper in the 1800s, sellers ripped a piece of paper from a single

41 Mount Desert Street (stop no. 9), Captain Benjamin Ash and Maria Ash graves in the Mount Desert Street Cemetery. *Courtesy of the author.*

sheet for a business transaction. The receipt would include the name of the payer or payee along with the amount, purpose and date. The receipts were all handwritten, which makes them hard to read in some cases, and some are on blue and other colored paper.

From 1842 to the end of the Civil War in 1865, there are only 32 receipts during this twenty-three-year period. From 1866 to Ash's death in 1882, there are 138, including 9 with no date but linked to Ash. His widow had another 15 from 1882 to 1885. There is a larger number of receipts after 1865 since Rockland and other coastal towns experienced a boom after the Civil War. These later receipts use more attractive stationery, which served as an advertisement for the company that provided the services.

One of the challenges to the twenty-first-century reader concerns the cost of items listed on these receipts from the Victorian era. To understand the receipts, a conversion to the modern buying power using a CPI Inflation Calculator[50] is necessary to provide a realistic value for the purchase. In other words, $1 in 1842 had the equivalent purchasing power of $31 in 2019, and in 1885, $1 had the purchasing power of $26.21 in 2019. These converted amounts using the specific year of the purchase are included in parentheses after the receipt amount to provide a better value of the purchase for the modern reader.

Captain Ash's father and grandfather, also named Benjamin Ash, were mariners living in the Sullivan/Gouldsboro area, where he began his career as a seaman as a young man. After Ash married Maria Higgins from Bar Harbor in 1838, the family remained living in Gouldsboro. By the 1840s, Ash had been hired as master for various vessels. The Maine Marine Museum in Bath reported that Ash was captain of four different vessels while he lived in Gouldsboro.[51] His first vessel was the *Governor Brooks*, a ninety-three-ton, two-masted schooner built in Lincolnville in 1817 and enrolled in Thomaston in 1844. The second ship was the *Orbit*, a schooner built in 1825 in Freeport and enrolled in Thomaston in 1845. Ash was commander and part owner of the *Leo*, an eighty-nine-ton, two-masted schooner built in Thomaston in 1823 and enrolled in Jonesboro in 1847. The fourth ship was the *Emblem*, a fifty-four-ton schooner built in Gloucester, Massachusetts, in 1825 and enrolled in 1849 in East Thomaston.

Thomaston, Maine, had a connection to all four of these vessels, which may have been due to its importance as a shipping building center and part of Maine's lime industry. Ash's receipts did not include any receipts from the city of Thomaston; however, the city was a close neighbor to the city of Rockland, and the lime industry was represented in multiple receipts. Captain Ash borrowed $1,000 ($31,000) from P. Pineo in 1847, which might have been related to his purchase of part ownership in the schooner *Leo*.[52] The Mystic Seaport Library has a record of Henry S. Cook as master of the *Leo* in 1854 and the ship being registered in Blue Hill.[53]

There is a gap in the information about Ash's employment from 1849 until the purchase nine years later of his most well-known schooner, *Glide*. Captain Ash listed his profession as "coaster" in the 1850 census, and he may have continued as master of the *Emblem* or another vessel before becoming the master and owner of *Glide*. This was an era when many mariners had part ownership of vessels. During this period, he moved his growing family to Eden (Bar Harbor). Penobscot Marine Museum records state that Ash was sole owner of *Glide* from 1858 to 1865. *Glide* was a fifty-two-ton two-masted schooner built in 1844 by N.M. Hall in Trenton.[54] Richard W. Hale Jr. mentioned the schooner *Glide* being owned by Ash in his 1949 book about Bar Harbor, noting that it was not built in Eden.[55] A receipt for a loan of $200 ($6,200.05) on February 10, 1858, from Edmund Higgins, a Trenton Point merchant, was most likely connected to the purchase or repair of the schooner *Glide* that year.

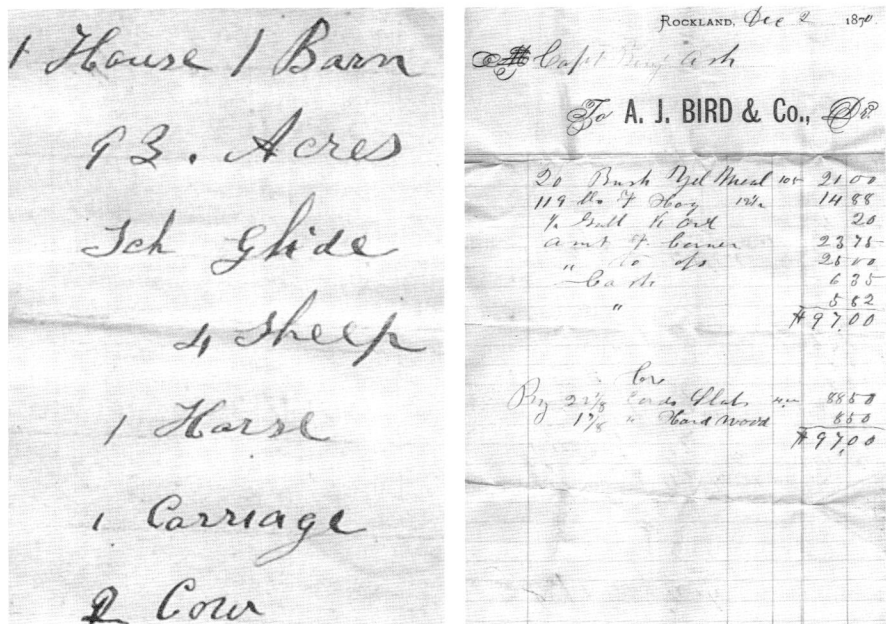

Left: Captain Ash receipt showing his 1870 assets for taxation. *Courtesy of the author.*

Right: Captain Ash receipt for A.J. Bird & Co., Rockland, 1870. *Courtesy of the author.*

Receipts in the collection show that Ash had at least partial ownership of *Glide* or was responsible for repairs of the ship until the early 1870s. The schooner was also listed on one of the receipts that recorded all of Captain Ash's assets in 1870.

A review of the U.S. census records during the latter part of Ash's life shows his continued career as a coaster. The 1860 U.S. census lists Ash's profession as a "seaman" and records that he owned $800 real estate and had a personal estate of $1,050 (including *Glide*). Ash called himself a "sea captain" in the 1870 U.S. census with $1,500 real estate and had a personal estate of $1,200 (including *Glide*). His sons, Alonzo, Orlando and Nathan, worked for him in the early 1870s, and their professions were listed as sailor, herring fisherman and sailor in the census, respectively. Orlando was also skilled at creating fishing seines.

The sixty-five-year-old Ash had no profession listed in the 1880 U.S. census; however, he did own the last of his vessels, the fifty-ton schooner *Priscilla Brown*, during this period of his life. The *Priscilla Brown* was built in Essex, Massachusetts, in 1848.[56] Essex was North America's center for

Captain Ash promissory note for Williams & Dean in 1876. *Courtesy of the author.*

fishing schooner construction in the 1800s, with fifteen shipyards that launched over four thousand vessels. A *Bar Harbor Mount Desert Herald* advertisement for the sale of the ship on March 22, 1883, after the death of Ash, stated that it had the capacity for twenty-five cords of wood, which suggests that firewood transportation was the service provided by the aging mariner. This schooner was sold by the estate to Captain David Bracy Jr. in May 1883 for $140 ($3,542.25), which was below the assessed value of $400 ($10,120.71) and designated $260 ($6,578.46) as a loss against the estate. Although Bracy was "fitting her up for the coasting business," the Mount Desert resident had many professions over the years, including cod fisherman, laborer and farmer, which could suggest that the length of his coaster career was short.[57] The *Priscilla Brown* was still in use twenty-three years later in 1906 and owned by an unnamed Southwest Harbor mariner.[58]

Several of Ash's receipts were related to the maintenance of his schooners, including the purchase of oars, sails, masts, anchors and other supplies. Ash bought an anchor from Jabez Simpson, a Sullivan merchant, who was his neighbor in 1846. Captain Ash had a large purchase in 1865 from Webb and Whitmore, fishing outfitters and the managing owners of fishing schooners from Oceanville on Deer Isle. This purchase may have been for a major ship renovation for *Glide* or another of his schooners, as that was their specialty. On April 27, 1867, Ash borrowed $218 ($3,744.33) in Rockland, Maine, for repairs on *Glide*. Rockland vendor Francis Harrington provided thirty-two-foot oars for $3.52 ($60.46) on June 15, 1867. There is a receipt for Robert Brewer Hamor in 1870 for $850 ($16,494.02) repairs for *Glide* performed by John Hopkins. Hamor was listed as a sea captain in 1860 and 1870 and a house and ship carpenter in 1880.

Captain Ash's receipts showed that he conducted most of his business in Rockland with two key merchants, Williams and Dean and A.J. Bird & Company. The Williams and Dean (Ephraim Dean and Benjamin Williams) receipts from 1845 to 1876 include six transactions ranging from $20 ($423.67) to $52.85 ($1,100.57). Items purchased by Ash include a one-hundred-pound box of herring, twenty-two cords of wood, thirty bushels of meal, flour, apples, tar, pitch and oats.

A.J. Bird & Company, located at 61 Front Street near Maverick Street and owned by Hanson G. Bird and Jackson Weeks, specialized in providing lime, groceries and dry goods. From 1867 to 1879, Ash had ten transactions with the company and purchases ranging from $3.85 ($97.87) to $97 ($1,882.26). Ash purchased seventeen casks of lime, rolls of paper and other household staples such as corn, flour, meal, molasses and tea from the company. The large number of casks of lime would suggest that lime transportation was a large part of Captain Ash's income during the 1860s and 1870s.

Three receipts in the collection are rare examples of payments to Captain Ash for services rendered. On October 14, 1861, Henry Hall paid Benjamin Ash $23.50 ($682.43) for fish accounts on demands and services rendered on board schooner *Glide* up to date. G.W. Higgins paid Benjamin Ash $11 ($179.05) on August 19, 1864, for "getting hay and putting on onboard." One other transaction involved Ash buying ten bags of corn in Rockland from A.J. Bird & Company for David Rodick of Bar Harbor. An Ellsworth receipt from September 26, 1868, was payment for six and a half cords of wood now in the hull of the schooner *Glide* and purchased of J.G. Aachen and signed by Judsonly Aachen. One receipt shows $8 ($199.37) payment for service by Clement Maning to Ash for chopping wood on January 18, 1880.

CAPTAIN FREDERICK ALLEN

During the time that Captain Benjamin Ash worked as a coaster, another unique mariner lived on the opposite side of the island. Captain Frederick Allen was the area's only African American resident for several decades. When Allen bought land on Spruce Point (later called Negro Point) in 1841, he became the first man or woman of African ancestry to own land on Mount Desert Island. Although Thomas Frazier in the late 1700s and early 1800s was considered the first free African American with an established residence in the area, he did not own the land where he lived and ran his

Captain Frederick Allen, African American mariner, 1870. *Courtesy of Ann Burns.*

saltworks to supply fishing schooners on Frazer Point (Schoodic Peninsula), which was supposedly named for a white London merchant named Thomas Frazer.[59] In 1780, Frazier enlisted in Captain Henry Dyer's company of rangers at Frenchman Bay in the Revolutionary War and raised a family of seven children.[60] Like Frazier's story, Frederick Allen's life on Mount Desert Island was unique for this time.

It is estimated that Black men made up a quarter of the mariners in the country before the Civil War, serving as cooks, stewards, sailmakers or caulkers. Blacks were often qualified for every station aboard a ship, but few of these men were allowed to command.[61] Allen may also have worked successfully at a variety of positions on a ship. His sons learned their skills from their father. Ivory became a steward, and Edward and Harvey were mariners. Frederick Jr. and George D. Allen became captains.

The Penobscot Marine Museum does not have a record of Allen owning a ship on Mount Desert Island during the 1800s.[62] Most Black mariners during this era did not own their own ships. Federal census records show that several Higgins family members were mariners, including his wife's brother Wyatt, who was lost at sea in 1869. Allen may have worked for the Higgins family or other ship owners from the Western Bay to accumulate the money that he reported in census and other records from 1840 to 1880.

Allen married a local girl, Climenia Higgins, but the marriage was not recognized in Maine since the legislature passed a law in 1821 that prohibited interracial marriage. In 1845, the Allen family appeared in the town records of Eden (Bar Harbor) with their children listed with no marriage date mentioned. Since common-law marriage is not recognized in Maine, the town seems to have looked the other way about the anti-miscegenation law once children were born. The couple had twelve children, with all living until adulthood.

Annetta "Nettie" Allen Higgins, Captain Allen's daughter, in the 1880s. *Courtesy of Ann Burns.*

Captain Allen's only surviving photograph shows a man of mixed races of his Scandinavian father and possibly Caribbean mother. The children of Captain Allen were noted in the census records as Black or mulatto while living in Maine. When they moved and settled in other states such as New Jersey, New York, Massachusetts and New Hampshire, they listed their race as white, and their children were considered white. Succeeding generations also continued to marry white women and men. Photos of the grandchildren and great-grandchildren of Captain Allen show people with little resemblance to him or his African heritage.

Captain Frederick Allen died on his farm on October 30, 1885, from a tumor. He was buried in his field on Spruce Point (Negro Point), which was a common practice at that time in West Eden. Although records at the Mountain View Cemetery state that his remains are buried there in his grave site, an inventory of the old burial grounds in West Eden by Eben M. Hamor on June 12, 1908, listed his graveyard as no. 7 and notes that it contains his remains. Old burial ground no. 6 contains the remains of his father-in-law and mother-in-law, John and Margaret Higgins, and others.

Captain Allen's son Charles Allen lived most of his adult life in Bar Harbor and Hulls Cove working as a laborer and gardener and then owned his own Hulls Cove farm. Charles married a widow, Julia Braley, from Waltham, Maine. His sister Virginia "Jennie" also lived in Bar Harbor and was married to Horace W. Jellison.

A clear understanding of what the Allen family meant to the community in West Eden is found in the obituary and tribute to Captain Allen's daughter Nettie C. Allen Higgins (Mrs. O.C. Higgins) when she died in 1915. Her obituary never mentions her family's race and instead states that she was a highly respected member of the community and that she was very active in the Mountain View Grange. Her memorial service was held at the Somesville Union Meeting House, conducted by Reverend Joseph N. Walker from Massachusetts. A week later, members of the grange posted a proclamation honoring Nettie, signed by grange officers and neighbors George W. Mayo, Minnie E. Hadley and Gertrude Clark. The proclamation stated that their charter was draped in mourning for thirty days to honor a "charter member and worthy sister."[63]

Bonus Historical Sites: Somesville Union Meeting House and the grave of Captain Frederick Allen in the Mountain View Cemetery.

Chapter 10

THE CHURCH LADY: ELIZABETH HIGGINS

ST. SAVIOUR'S EPISCOPAL CHURCH AND RECTORY
41 MOUNT DESERT STREET

A recent visitor to Bar Harbor, George Marcou, was immediately drawn to the beautiful wood and stone English Gothic St. Saviour's Episcopal Church with its Tiffany stained-glass windows and its Queen Anne–style rectory. The church was named after the French Jesuit mission St. Saveur that was established on the western shore of Somes Sound in an area now known as Fernald's Point in the town of Southwest Harbor in 1613. The original building was completed in 1878 and seated 325 people. The church was expanded to accommodate its growing congregation. Mrs. William Vanderbilt built a Sunday school hall in 1888. The chancel and sanctuary were added in 1900, and the style of the church was said to have changed from Victorian Gothic to Romanesque Revival with Shingle elements and a seating capacity of 800.[64] Marcou was particularly enchanted by the Tiffany stained-glass windows, which were given to the church by L.C. Tiffany, a summer resident for several years who attended the church. These windows memorialize several prominent parishioners. The altar in the church was donated by Mrs. Ogden in memory of her husband, Gouverneur Morris Ogden of New York, who died in 1884. St. Saviour's Episcopal Church is the oldest, largest and tallest public building on Mount Desert Island, and the National Register of Historic Places recognizes the church and the rectory.

A large plaque in the south transept (right wing) of St. Saviour's Episcopal Church provides a tribute to Elizabeth "Lizzie" Higgins, who worked tirelessly in the early days of the church from the late 1870s until her sudden passing on November 7, 1913, from a heart attack. Along with her two sisters,

41 Mount Desert Street (stop no. 10), St. Saviour's Episcopal Church and Rectory, has a plaque commemorating Elizabeth Higgins. *Courtesy of the author.*

Adeline Higgins and Mariam Roberts, she was a fixture in the church. The plaque on the wall of the church reads:

> *To the Glory of God*
> *And in loving Memory of*
> *Elizabeth Higgins*
> *1844–1913*
> *A member of the First Confirmation*
> *Class in St. Saviors Church*
> *And the First Choir*
> *Faithful Unto Death*
> *"The souls of the righteous are in the hands of God and there shall no torment touch them."*

Elizabeth "Lizzie" was one of the nine children of Benjamin and Maria (Mariah) Ash. She married Ambrose Higgins, a house carpenter, in 1866, and they lived on a property next to Ambrose's father. Daniel Higgins, a ship carpenter, and his mother, Hannah (née Higgins), who lived on Atlantic Avenue. Daniel Higgins's real estate assets were valued at $1,500 in 1870.

The house where Ambrose and Elizabeth lived was on a private lane called Locust Lane, named after the locust trees (Gleditsia) along the road. The road was parallel to Atlantic Avenue and the future Derby Lane. Their house (6 Locust Lane) was said to be two houses that were joined together, with at least one of the buildings being moved to the location by a team of horses. During the 1890s and early 1900s, part of the house was rented to summer residents and called the Ambrose Higgins Cottage.

Another property owned by the couple and located on their land closer to the ocean was called the Baltimore Cottages. After Dr. Hasket Derby, one of the founders of the ophthalmology profession in America, built his new house, Shore Acres, he sold his two older existing cottages built in the 1870s to Ambrose Higgins. In the fall of 1882, the two buildings were moved to the Higgins property and became the Baltimore Cottage 1 and 2. The Higgins family consistently rented out these buildings to summer visitors from the 1880s until the 1940s. At some point after 1916 and before the late 1940s, the building closest to Main Street was torn down, and the other property, which was said to have once been a carriage house, was sold to Raymond Turner in 1951.

After Ambrose Higgins rebuilt 6 Locust Lane in 1904, Elizabeth established a maternity hospital in one of the Higgins buildings for local women who were not allowed to use Mount Desert Island Hospital to have their babies during the summer season. Her granddaughter Carolyn E. Higgins had a successful nursing career that was inspired by both her mother, Georgia Tripp Higgins, and her grandmother's work at the maternity hospital.[65] A story about an orphaned baby being left at the door of the Moseley Cottage on Atlantic Avenue (aka the Poplars) on Christmas morning, a stone's throw from the Higgins hospital, suggests that Elizabeth may have been involved in the adoption of the child by Ellen "Ellie" F. Moseley.[66] The Higgins maternity hospital continued to deliver babies for at least ten years after Elizabeth's death, which included Tom Testa's mother, Eleanor Moran Testa, who was born there on October 26, 1922. Other birthing centers on Mount Desert Island in the early twentieth century included the Sprague (lower Main Street), Cunningham (Hulls Cove), Webber or Dingville (Ledgelawn Extension) and Rich (Somesville) maternity hospitals. The maternity ward at MDI Hospital was not completed until 1939, and summer residents' animals were given preference to local people during the season for X-rays and other medical services at the hospital before World War II.

Elizabeth Higgins was very active in the newly established St. Saviour's Episcopal Church. As the plaque mentioned, she was a member of the

first confirmation class at St. Saviour's, the first choir and the Ladies' Auxiliary. Elizabeth was a charter member of the Ladies Aid Society in Bar Harbor, which worked to promote industry and to aid in all good work. The group worked closely with BHVIA, and one of its achievements was to buy the town's first hearse in 1883.[67] She also bought a house on Davis Place for her sister Julia Ells when her family experienced hard times and homelessness.

Elizabeth was one of the year-round residents who were financially successful and enjoyed entertaining. She, along with her two sisters, Mrs. W.M. Roberts (Mariam) and Mrs. Edwin Higgins (Adeline), took buckboard drives on the new Sargeant Drive by Somes Sound, hosted teas and parties and went on shopping excursions by steamship to Boston. The guests of her parties and tea attendees were all from prominent permanent resident families of the island.

Elizabeth and Ambrose had two sons, Clinton Bird and Edward "Leander." Clinton, an avid sportsman, was involved in the harness and saddlery business on Cottage Street with Nathan Ash and later owned a candy store in town. After his father, Ambrose, died in 1910, he moved his family from 216 Main Street to live with Elizabeth. She passed three years later in 1913, and Clinton managed the family properties and continued to live at 6 Locust Lane with his family until his death in 1918. His widow, Georgia, later married Dr. Royal Grant Higgins in the late 1920s.

Top: Elizabeth Higgins in the early 1900s. *Courtesy of Sally Higgins Pim.*

Bottom: Elizabeth Higgins's granddaughter Carolyn E. Higgins. *Courtesy of David Higgins.*

His brother, E. Leander Higgins, became prominent architect in Maine. As a young man, he was a member of the Pemetic Ice Yacht Club and won several awards for his yacht the *Beagle*, built by his father, Ambrose, which was sailed by John W. Roberts.[68] Following his graduation from Bar Harbor High School, E. Leander went to Boston, where he worked for architect Guy Lowell and attended Massachusetts Institute of Technology. After graduation in 1905, he relocated to Portland and became a partner in the firm of Burnham and Higgins. He designed many Maine buildings, including the Immanuel Baptist Church in Portland, St. Thomas Episcopal Church in Camden and many residences in the Portland area. Higgins was often employed by the City of Portland and by the State of Maine and drew the plans for the State Reformatory for Women at Skowhegan. He became a member of the Maine Society of the Sons of the American Revolution in 1916, tracking his ancestry on the Higgins side to Israel Higgins II (1728–1818), who was a volunteer in Captain Daniel Sullivan's company during the unsuccessful Penobscot Expedition in 1779.

His son, Ambrose Higgins, was also a successful architect in Maine for many years. After graduating from the School of Architecture at the Massachusetts Institute of Technology in 1935, he joined his father's firm, and they established their Bar Harbor office in the Baltimore Cottage. His father passed in 1936, and Ambrose opened an office at 200 Main Street in the English Shops after serving in the U.S. Air Force in World War II. He left Bar Harbor in 1952 to work for Crowell-Lancaster—later known as Crowell-Lancaster-Higgins and then Higgins-Webster & Partners—in Bangor. Higgins's design work included "a wide variety of buildings including residential, commercial, industrial, educational and public structures."[69]

Ambrose was involved in the design of the renovation of the Casino as a theater for Broadway-quality plays in 1947 and the Ethel I. Conners Elementary School in Bar Harbor. A collection of both the father's and son's drawings and papers is archived at the University of Maine Library in Orono.

Locust Lane was featured on old maps but disappeared after Derby Lane became a town road. The two renovated cottages from 1904 survive today as the Derby Lane Cottage at 6 Derby Lane, which consists of the Arbor House (the Higgins family home for many years) and the Stork's Nest (the maternity hospital run by Elizabeth and later a rental property). One of the Baltimore Cottage buildings survives today as 1 Elbow Lane. The other Baltimore Cottage building closest to Main Street was torn down by the

Higgins family and replaced by a house and garage in 1959 by Michele Testa. Haskett Derby's cottage Shore Acres, designed by William Ralph Emerson and built in 1881, was torn down in 1957, and the foundation survives near the Shore Path.

Bonus Historical Site: The Bar Harbor Congregational Church (29 Mount Desert Street) is located on the site of the original Union Meeting House or "White Church," as it was commonly called. This building was used for all Protestant religious services until each denomination built its own building. The Union Meeting House was purchased and replaced by the Bar Harbor Congregational Church in 1883. The church burned in 1942 and was replaced on November 7, 1951, by the present structure, which was designed to look like the old White Church.

Bonus Historical Site: The Eden Civil War Monument, located in the middle of the Mount Desert Street Cemetery, was designed and built by Cook & Watkins of Boston with granite supplied by N.H. Higgins of Ellsworth. It was dedicated on November 4, 1897, after a $4,500 contribution from the Town of Bar Harbor and $500 from public subscription. The monument inscription reads: "In Memory of Eden's Sons Who Were Defenders of the Union 1861–1865."

One of the most revered Civil War veterans from Eden (Bar Harbor) was William B. Campbell. An 1897 *Bar Harbor Record* article includes a story from Eban M. Hamor about Campbell's return to Maine after being wounded in a Civil War battle. Campbell enlisted in Company G, Maine Twenty-Second Infantry Regiment, on October 10, 1862, at the age of nineteen, and his unit traveled to Louisiana, where they participated in the efforts to capture Port Hudson, an important location on the Mississippi River. Sometime before July 7, Campbell was seriously wounded and had his leg amputated. His health was so bad that he was not able to return to Eden (Bar Harbor) when his unit mustered out on August 14 and instead had to go to the hospital in Augusta.

When Hamor visited him, Campbell pleaded with him to take him home. The hospital said that the trip would kill him; however, Hamor agreed to take him. The two men traveled north for serval days to return home. People they met along the way made sure that Campbell's trip was "safe and comfortable," which mimicked "the feeling all over the country" that "nothing was too good for the soldier." When it seemed that Campbell was dying, he was asked if he regretted enlisting in the army, and the veteran replied that "he had never seen a moment yet when he was sorry that he had volunteered." Campbell returned to Eden (Bar Harbor), healed and married widow Abbie Marie Liscomb Emery on October 11, 1872. They lived in Ellsworth with her daughter Olive Emery. He became a blacksmith and later was the register of deeds for Hancock County for several decades. Campbell died in Ellsworth in 1906 at the age of sixty-three.

Chapter 11

THE MISSES SHANNON

LEDGELAWN INN
66 MOUNT DESERT STREET

In the latter part of the nineteenth century, the Misses Shannon had a lasting impact on the village of Eden (Bar Harbor). Although Mary Clarke Shannon ("Mary Sr.") and her niece Mary Shannon ("Mary Jr.") were considered part of the elite summer colony, their "love for and interest in Bar Harbor welfare was great and enduring."[70] Previously published books about Bar Harbor have neglected to discuss the lives of these fascinating women. The pair were involved in all the key movements of their era, including African American education, women's suffrage, prohibition, animal rights, women's health, transcendentalism, art education, free libraries and recreational land preservation. Bar Harbor benefited from their philanthropy, which included the donation of Glen Mary Park, financial support for the Bar Harbor Free Library, development of the Ledgelawn neighborhood, land for the Unitarian church and funding and land for the BHVIA.

The family fortune was established when Mary Clarke Shannon's brother Oliver N. Shannon moved to Boston from New Hampshire and became a successful businessman. He married Harriet M. Burlen in Saco, Maine, in 1835, and the couple continued to reside in Boston, where their first child, Mary Shannon, was born on September 19, 1836. The marriage produced two more children, with only Mary surviving to adulthood.

After living in other parts of Boston for several years, the Shannons bought a large thirty-acre plot of land at 749 Center Street in Newton Center, Newton, in 1840, which included the 1798 three-story "fine old house" made of "brick and clapboard" designed by Charles Bulfinch and

66 Mount Desert Street (stop no. 11), the house built by J.E. Clark for S.W. Bridgham in 1904 to replace the 1870s Shannon cottage and later called the Ledgelawn Inn. *Courtesy of the author.*

built by Joseph Blake of Boston on the west side from Cabot Street on Center Street, which earlier in the century was called Sargent Place.[71] The property also included "a greenhouse and box-bordered gardens laid in the style of Mount Vernon."[72] Oliver invited his mother and sister to move into the house in 1842, and it became the house of three generations of Mary Shannons for twenty years.

After the death of the younger children, the marriage was strained, which was reflected in Massachusetts court proceedings in the 1850s and 1860s. Harriet claimed she moved out of the house around 1846 due to cruelty from her husband, and Oliver claimed she deserted the family and was an unfit mother. Legal documents claim that Oliver's mother and sister had disputes with his wife in the house. Passages in young Mary's journal from 1853 show the level of tension between her two parents. In 1855, Oliver took his nineteen-year-old daughter to Terre Haute, Indiana, to establish residence there, as he was unable to divorce Harriet in Massachusetts. On September 15, 1856, Mary noted in her journal, "Father is divorced. Last Monday."[73] Harriet sought to reconcile and/or sue for separate maintenance but was unsuccessful in these actions. Newspapers and other court documents provide information about the divorce and Harriet's attempts to invalidate the legal action.[74] Oliver Shannon prevailed in the ensuing legal battles in an era when women rarely won in court actions.

Oliver Shannon passed away on December 25, 1869, from apoplexy at the age of fifty-seven and was buried in Mount Auburn Cemetery in Cambridge, Massachusetts. His will was registered in Indiana to protect his fortune from his ex-wife. Oliver Shannon's estate went primarily to his daughter, Mary, with generous annual annuities to his living siblings, including Mary C. Shannon, Isaac Shannon, William Shannon and Mrs. Higgins. His assets were invested in Commonwealth of Massachusetts bonds and City of Boston bonds for the development and improvement of the city real estate. The Newton house, all the furnishings, buildings and farm equipment from the thirty-two-acre farm went to Mary Jr., along with a $2,000-per-year annuity.

Mary Clarke Shannon (Mary Sr.) was active in the issues of the day, including abolition of slavery, helping the poor and women's suffrage. She was said to be "a noble and philanthropic woman conspicuous in all good deed and lovely charities."[75] Famous nineteenth-century writer, reformer and philanthropist Ednah Dow Cheney said that she was the "rarest and

Old Ledge Lawn cottage built by the Shannons in 1870s. *Courtesy of the Bar Harbor Historical Society.*

noblest type of women," and "humanity in every form was dear to her."[76] She was an important part of the group of charitable women involved in the cause of women's suffrage that included Elizabeth Cady Stanton, Isabella Beecher Hooker and others.[77]

Mary Sr. was also an active abolitionist. A recent sale of a letter addressed to her from abolitionist Caroline Severance was sent with a gift of a fragment of wood, identified as a piece of the gallows on which John Brown was hanged, which showed her involvement with the movement.[78] Severance was also active in the women's suffrage movement.

The elder Miss Shannon had the biggest influence on the education and character development of her niece, who attended West Newton English and Classical School. The Misses Shannon worked together on various charitable projects. In 1872, the Shannons helped establish the Rebecca Pomroy Newton Home for Orphan and Destitute Girls. The school was named for their close family friend and tutor to the children of Abraham Lincoln. The school was chartered as the Rebecca Pomroy Newton Home for Orphan Girls in 1884 with a mission to "care for, train, and educate destitute and orphan girls, and aid them in procuring means of self-support."[79] The organization later expanded to provide educational and recreational services to people of all ages in the community under the name of the Rebecca Pomroy Foundation.[80]

The Misses Shannon first visited Bar Harbor in 1865 for a two-week vacation. In 1871, they returned for the summer, and after that, they visited every summer. In 1876, they purchased seventy acres of land and built the Shingle-style cottage Ledge Lawn on Mount Desert Street. The architect was probably W. Jordan, who was also the contractor. The land was in a sheltered position that protected it from the cold northerly wind by the elevation of the ridge along Mount Desert Street and by the hills from the westerly winds, making it "a very desirable retreat, in winter; and its beautiful surroundings and retired position render it a delightful location in summer."[81]

The 1881 Colby map shows the Shannon property, including the Exchange Hotel, owned by Mr. and Mrs. Willard C. Higgins. The hotel had a capacity for forty visitors and was the

Mary Shannon, who was called Mary Jr., 1880s. *Courtesy of David Wingate Seavey.*

Mary Clark Shannon, who was called Mary Sr., 1880s. *Courtesy of David Wingate Seavey.*

only year-round hotel in town during this era catering to local businessmen and off-season visitors. George Grant recalled in 1904 that the hotel was "a trifle cool for us that winter there being, aside from the kitchen stove, only a small air-tight in one room, which was supposed to warm the whole house."[82] The hotel was sold to J. Watson in 1886 and moved to West Street near Rodick Street. The land that the hotel occupied was incorporated into the Ledge Lawn grounds, which included the cottage and a studio that were separated by a grand looping driveway.

Like many summer visitors at that time, the Shannons arrived after July 4. In 1881, they followed their normal pattern of staying at the St. Sauveur Hotel while their cottage was being opened for the season. They were called cottage boarders. When the St. Sauveur Hotel burned in October 1881, the cottage of the Misses Shannon on the opposite side of Mount Desert Street was in dangerous proximity to the burned building, but it was watched by men on the roof who kept it well wetted down.[83]

In 1882, the two ladies arrived on Thursday, July 20, by the steamer *Mount Desert*. They lived in their cottage until late October, when they "left for their winter home."[84] By 1885, the name of the Shannon cottage in Bar Harbor was Ledge Lawn.

After the passing of her aunt on August 19, 1887, in Newton at the age of seventy-three, Mary Jr. became more active in Bar Harbor with philanthropy.

She was a "great admirer of Theodore Parker," the famous Unitarian minister. After "the orthodox society closed the doors of the Union church in Bar Harbor to the Unitarians, because of their non-evangelical belief," Mary Jr. gave a lot of her land on Ledgelawn Avenue to the church and paid $5,000 to "build on it a church dedicated for all time to liberal preaching."[85] This church served Bar Harbor Unitarians until the 1970s, when it was torn down and replaced with a home. Mary Jr. added an addition to the Shannon cottage, Ledge Lawn, in 1888.

Mary Jr. helped develop Ledgelawn Avenue by encouraging development on or near her land. Along with these efforts, she donated the land for the Glen Mary Park, which she saw as a children's park. She offered to build a town hall on Ledgelawn Avenue if she could pick the architect/builder; however, the town rejected the offer. She supported the BHVIA and the Bar Harbor Free Library, and they later received $4,000 and $1,000, respectively, in her will. During the 1890s, the Indian village of the Passamaquoddy tribe moved from the waterfront to Ledgelawn Avenue.

In the mid-1890s, Mary Jr. did not come to Maine that summer since she was traveling in the South in 1894 and 1895, visiting Tuskegee and Hampton Institutes, with Julia Ward Howe, Ednah Dow Cheney and Alice Stone Blackwell. She also met with Booker T. Washington on this trip. Washington visited Bar Harbor in the late 1880s and visited Ledge Lawn.[86]

In 1900, Mary Jr. lived in Newton with her two nieces, Sarah Pearson Wingate and Mary Shannon Wingate; Mary McClellan (twenty-five), cook; Betty Peterson (twenty-four), servant; and Michael Leonard (thirty-five), coachman. She summered in Bar Harbor with at least one of the nieces each year. Like her father, Mary Jr. prepared her will a few years before her death and filed it in a state outside of her home state of Massachusetts. Her estate was worth $750,000 in 1901 ($22,596,352.94 in 2019).

Mary Shannon (Mary Jr.) died suddenly on April 19, 1901, at her home in Newton of heart failure, and a message came to Ben Hadley, who was caretaker of her property in Bar Harbor. Newspapers reported that she had been out riding with Mr. and Mrs. Prescott Cleaves only the previous Tuesday and "was then in her usual health and spirits."[87] The newspaper notice said that "she was 63 years old though her hair had been white for five years."[88] Funeral services were held in Newton. Her obituary in the *Bar Harbor Record* recalled:

> *Her patriotism was displayed when she presented the town the first flags that were raised on the school buildings. She was widely known as a*

philanthropist and gave largely her money for charitable and educational purposes. But always quietly and without publicity. Those loved her best knew her best. Her loss will be greatly felt by many in Bar Harbor.[89]

The largest amounts of inheritance went to her two nieces, Sarah Pearson Wingate and Mary Shannon Wingate, who received $75,000 ($2,259,635.29 in 2019) and $50,000 ($1,506,423.53 in 2019), respectively. They also received use of her house in Newton, jewelry and household items. Their mother, Sarah Ann Wingate, received $50,000 ($1,506,423.53 in 2019) to use for the farm in Hampton, New Hampshire. To honor the wishes of her father, she made sure to provide money to surviving family members connected to Oliver's siblings and friends' children.

Institutions receiving money in Mary Shannon's will included Wellesley College scholarships ($15,000), Tuskegee Normal Industrial School for Negroes ($5,000), Kittrall Normal Industrial School for Negroes ($5,000), Atlanta University for Colored Students Endowment ($5,000), Massachusetts SPCA ($2,000), Women's Education and Industrial Union ($2,000), NE Women's Suffrage Association ($2,000), American Purity Alliance Association of New York City ($2,000), Newton City Hospital ($10,000), Rebecca Pomroy ($10,000), Newton Library ($5,000), Newton Firemen's Relief Fund ($3,300), North East Hospital for Women and Children at Boston Highlands ($10,000), Hampton Normal School, Hampton, Virginia ($10,000) and the School for Poor Whites in Kinsy, Alabama ($5,000).

Her nieces showed little interest in the Bar Harbor property, and the estate quickly sold Ledge Lawn and subdivided the property. The house was torn down and replaced with a new home built by J.E. Clark for S.W. Bridgham in 1904. To honor her long-term caretaker, Benjamin Hadley, Mary gave him $10,000 to buy a house. Shortly after the will was resolved, he received his check and bought 62 Ledgelawn Avenue, which was built in 1895 at the intersection of Pleasant Street and Ledgelawn Avenue. The family lived in this house for the next half century.

Mary Jr. stipulated in her will that the two nieces, Sarah Pearson Wingate and Mary Shannon Wingate, could remain in the Newton house as long they lived, with the estate paying $2,000 a year to maintain it. On March 1, 1905, in Newton, Sarah Pearson Wingate married thirty-seven-year-old Harry Melville Taylor, the brother of an artist whom Mary Jr. helped with money in her will. Taylor was from an old Boston family that dated back to the Pilgrims and owned land on Clark's Island.

The two nieces remained living together in the house until 1916. The executors of the estate wanted to eliminate the ongoing annual cost to maintain the estate by selling the property. In May 1916, the executor of the will sold 29.5 acres to a buyer, Loren D. Towle, a prominent real estate executive, philanthropist and city activist. Part of the sale included the 3.5 acres where the house and garden were located. In September 1916, Mrs. Taylor (Sarah Pearson Wingate) transferred to Towle all her interest in the premises, voiding her life guarantee to the property. Towle sued Mary Shannon Wingate so that she would also leave. She refused, won the case in court and remained in the house for the next thirty years until her death. The property owners, Newton Country Day School, razed the house, which ended the physical presence of the Shannons in Newton.

The BHVIA installed a bench in honor of Mary Shannon Jr. in the Glen Mary Park in 2014. The Bridgham cottage was used as a bed-and-breakfast called the Ledgelawn Inn for many years. It was bought by Ocean Properties in 2011 and has been used as employee housing for its hotels.

Other Mount Desert Street Sites: Old YMCA/Abbe Museum (26 Mount Desert Street, 1900); Jesup Memorial Library (34 Mount Desert Street, 1911); YWCA (36 Mount Desert Street, 1913); Stratford House Inn/the Poplars (45 Mount Desert Street, 1900); Thornridge Inn (47 Mount Desert Street, 1900); Marcyes Cottage (48 Mount Desert Street, 1886); Holy Redeemer Roman Catholic Church (56 Mount Desert Street, 1907); and Christian Science Church/White Columns (57 Mount Desert Street, 1937).

Chapter 12
OLDEST COTTAGE ON MOUNT DESERT STREET

STONE THROW COTTAGE INN AND MIRA MONTE INN 67 AND 69 MOUNT DESERT STREET

A friendly debate over the designation as the oldest surviving cottage on Mount Desert Street has been discussed for decades between the owners of the Mira Monte and the Stone Throw Cottage Inns. During a renovation of the Mira Monte in the late 1970s, a board stamped with the date 1868 led the owner, Marian Stanley Burns, to believe that the house was built that year. The Stone Throw Cottage Inn owners refuted this claim by providing old photos from the mid-1870s that showed only a barn on the property.

Further research into real estate records revealed that Orlando Ash bought the Mira Monte property from his father, Benjamin Ash, and then decided to expand his property and begin construction of the great house in 1879. The 1880 map shows both the right and left wings of the Mira Monte completed. Bar Harbor builders in the late 1870s recycled wood from older dwellings, which could explain the dated board from an old barn.

Once the property was completed, the story goes that Rachel Ash felt the house was too difficult to heat in the winter and asked Orlando to build a smaller and warmer house behind it. The new house, built in June 1887 by A.S. Bunker, builder of the St. Sauveur Hotel, would later lead to the development of Ash Place. Orlando later built a house for each of his two children, Ollie Getchell and John Ash, next to his property on Ash Place.

Orlando Ash rented the house, called the Orlando Ash cottage, out for a few seasons from 1883 to 1892. He first rented the house out in 1883 to U.S. senator Eugene Hale. The barn behind the house was replaced

This page: 67 and 69 Mount Desert Street (stop no. 12), Stone Throw Cottage Inn and Mira Monte Inn. *Courtesy of the author.*

by the servants' quarters when the property was rented to James Blaine, U.S. senator from Maine, in 1884. Blaine was running for president that year and was one of Maine's most prominent citizens. Other renters of the cottage included James P. Scott of Philadelphia, who owned railroad, oil and coal companies; Dr. K.D. Chaney from South Manchester (1887);

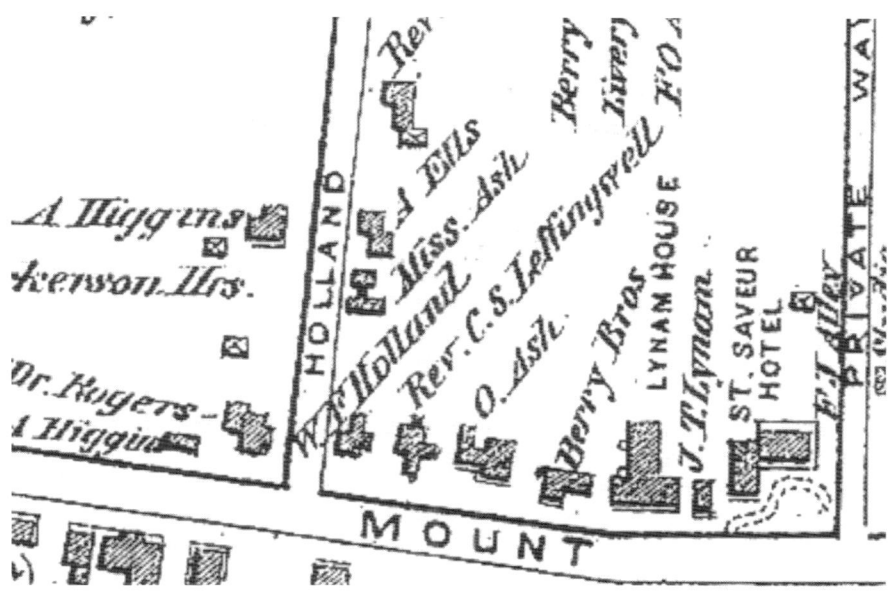

Map showing Mount Desert Street and Holland Avenue in the early 1880s. *Courtesy of the author.*

Orlando Ash, who built the Mira Monte cottage, with his son John Ash in the 1890s. *Courtesy of the author.*

Philadelphia banker and broker W.H. Gaw (1888–89); and George A. Robbins from New York (1890–91).

The Chapmans bought the Orlando Ash cottage in September 1892. They owned it for thirty-nine years and called the cottage the Mira Monte. Dr. Henry C. Chapman was the curator of the Academy of Natural Sciences in Philadelphia for thirty-four years and "made many valuable studies of the fauna and flora and deep sea life along the Maine coast."[90] He died in 1909, and his wife continued the role of hostess for many years. The house was given to Marie Ringgold Robins and her husband, Thomas, when Helen Chapman died on Christmas Day 1931.

The Robins family had the property until 1946, when they sold it to Edward Wilson, who then sold the property to the Robinson brothers (Leslie and Lawrence). Leslie Robinson was the husband of Aquaie White Robinson, who was the grandniece of Orlando Ash. The Robinsons quickly sold the property to Marion Bonnell on August 4, 1947.

The Bonnell family also purchased the Leffingwell Rectory (1880s) property between the Mira Monte and the Primrose. The Bonnell family owned the property until the death of Marion Bonnell in 1969. Her husband, Ward, sold the property to Chauncey McFarland in 1971. McFarland also owned the Nathan Ash cottage (Holbrook House) across Mount Desert Street.

McFarland sold the Mira Monte property to Bernard and Elsie Dowd in the late 1970s, and they sold it to Marian Burns in 1980. In the history of the house, Marian had the property for thirty-five years and the Chapmans had it for thirty-nine years. Both the Chapmans and Marian owned it longer than Orlando Ash, who only had the house for about thirteen years.

Although Gladys O'Neal and others dated the Stone Throw Cottage Inn as circa 1860 and stated that the Berry brothers built the cottage, this is not possible, since the Berry brothers, Fred H. and Chas. H., were still living with their successful father, John Berry, owner of a profitable stable in Rockland, Maine, that year. This property was originally owned by Oliver Higgins, who built a homestead on the property for his wife and seven children during the 1850s on Up the Road Street, which would later be called Mount Desert Street. Higgins owned other local properties, including Long Porcupine and the Hop, in the 1850s and early 1860s. He and his son-in-law Benjamin Ash used these lands for haying, sheep grazing, logging and drying fish.[91]

After Oliver Higgins died in 1862 at the age of eighty-six, his wife, Rhoda, and two daughters Rhoda II and Sally continued to live with her in the house. Rhoda II died August in 1871 at age fifty-nine, and her mother died in September 1871 at age eighty-nine. Sally, the last living Higgins family member living in the house, died in 1876. The property was then sold by the surviving heirs to Oliver Higgins's grandson Nathan Ash in April 1876. He sold the property to William F. Holland in December 1878. On May 6, 1880, Holland sold the property to Amos Crocket of Rockland, and Crocket sold it to the Berry brothers two months later, on June 24, 1880.

The Berry brothers' main interest in the property was the Cottage Street stable, which provided livery and hack with single or double teams. Their specialty was taking care of "boarded and transient horses."[92] They added dormers and a front porch to the cottage, which Fred H. Berry used as a summer residence. When the Bar Harbor real estate market began to heat up in the early 1880s, they sold the property.

The Berry brothers sold the property to wealthy Philadelphia merchant, broker and real estate developer Edward Samuel on September 25, 1885, for $11,000.[93] Samuel, the son of a Jewish fur dealer who emigrated from England, spent twenty-four seasons in Bar Harbor before his purchase and was considered one of the "original cottagers."[94] In 1886, Samuel transformed the humble Higgins cottage into a residence worthy of a Victorian gentleman. The first phase involved a complete renovation of most of the house. Samuel may have kept the outside walls and the floors, but everything else changed except for the original cellar, which was only under the right side of the house. The roof was significantly changed as more space was added on the second floor of the building. A.S. Bunker performed the renovations.

Two years later, in 1888, Samuel built the tower on the southwest corner of the cottage. It was the tower that gave the cottage the nickname "the bedbug cottage" from the locals, who did not like the tower and said it made the building look like the dreaded bug. After completion of the renovations and tower addition, Samuel and his wife visited each summer and usually included his wife's nieces the Misses Evans, Mary and Josephine Evans, as their house guests for the season.

In March 1892, Anne Russell Samuel died in Philadelphia at the age of forty-eight. Her death was a huge loss to Samuel, and he did not spend the summer in Bar Harbor for the next two seasons. The *Bar Harbor Record* reported on June 9, 1892, that Samuel came to town briefly to rent "his cottage for the season and will not tarry with us this year."

The newspaper accounts of the summer 1894 season showed a return to Samuel summering for the season with the Misses Evans. What was not revealed was the blossoming romance between the fifty-year-old

Edward Samuel and his deceased wife's twenty-two-year-old niece, Mary Campbell Evans. After the end of the Bar Harbor season, the two married in the closing months of 1894. When they returned for the summer season, Samuel's new young wife was expecting a child, and the family remained in Bar Harbor until Edward Samuel Jr. was born at the cottage on September 21, 1895. When mother and child were strong enough, the family returned to Philadelphia in October by train.

Samuel and his business partner, William Selfridge, had big plans for 1896. They formed the Maine Company and bought large tracts of land in Pretty Marsh and Trenton to develop that part of the island with multiple cottages. They had $100,000 capital stock and planned to begin work in 1896. Samuel was also having a cottage built on the western side of the island in Pretty Marsh.

In late March, residents in Bar Harbor learned of the sudden death of Edward Samuel after "a brief illness of pneumonia" on March 27. The paper added that the "very portly gentleman weigh[ed] over 260 pounds" and "always enjoyed good health" and was "quite wealthy."[95] The business plans were canceled, and Selfridge and others were put in charge of his estate to assist his wife and son. Samuel assigned most of the estate to raise his son, along with a percentage of the trust for Mary's expenses, with the stipulation that if she remarried, her percentage from the trust would be reduced. Mrs. Samuel and her son spent the 1896 and 1897 seasons in Bar Harbor at the Lynam House (1870s) run by John Lynam and his wife. By 1898, Mary was back spending the summer in the cottage and was well connected to the summer colony.

In January 1899, the newspapers reported an "engagement of unusual interest to the people of Bar Harbor's summer colony" of Mary C. Samuel to Mr. Lewis R. Ashhurst Jr., whose father was Dr. Francis Ashhurst from Mount Holly, New Jersey. His uncle Richard was an attorney, and his uncle Lewis, who was wounded at Gettysburg, was appointed postmaster of Philadelphia by President Theodore Roosevelt. Lewis's grandfather, also named Lewis R. Ashhurst, had been a wealthy retail import merchant.

The engagement announcement said that Mary was "a young matron who moves in the most select social circles in Bar Harbor and Philadelphia" and owned "a beautiful cottage on Mount Desert street in this village, where she spends the summer." After the marriage, the couple had a daughter, and they continued to come to Bar Harbor, using the tower wing as a place for the children and the nanny. After a few years, the couple stopped coming to Bar Harbor, and the cottage was used as an investment.

The Ashhurst marriage had difficulties, and they divorced in the late 1910s. For several years, Mary did not spend any time at the cottage. The newspaper in 1915 made a big deal about her occupying the cottage that season with her two children. Surviving photos of Mary suggest that she may have experienced a disfiguring accident or illness during this period. In 1917, Mary was given full ownership of the cottage, and the Cottage Street portion of the property was sold to John Peters. In 1919, she first called the cottage the Kare Free. This name was used numerous times over the next twenty-seven years to describe the cottage and her stays at the property.

Mary sold the property to Albert Eugene Gallatin in 1946, eight years before her death in 1954 at the age of eighty-two. Gallatin, who summered in Bar Harbor for decades, staying at the Malvern Hotel (1882) and St. Sauveur Hotel (1870), was a tenant of the cottage that summer before the purchase. He was born in 1881 in Villanova, Pennsylvania, from a distinguished family whose ancestry included Albert Gallatin, secretary of the treasury under Thomas Jefferson and founder of New York University. Gallatin, "a leading proponent of nonobjective and later abstract and particularly Cubist art,"[96] was an influential writer; art collector and exhibitor; and abstract painter who made frequent trips to Paris, where he visited Picasso, Georges Braque, Henri Matisse and other avant-garde artists in their studios and purchased works directly from them.[97] In 1919, he published the book *Art and the Great War* (1919), in which he "discussed war-related art in the allied nations, giving many examples of paintings, drawings, posters, caricatures, and prints that he admired."[98] Albert Gallatin renamed the cottage "the Mount," added a sundial to the front lawn of the house that was a familiar local landmark and made other physical changes to the cottage.

Gallatin died on June 15, 1952, at Chestnut Hill, Philadelphia, and the Jesup Memorial Library had an exhibit of his non-objective paintings in the summer of 1953 as tribute to the artist who had been the chairman of the exhibits committee of the library for many years. His paintings were displayed in New York, Paris, Honolulu, San Francisco, Chicago, Seattle and Boston and are owned by the Metropolitan Museum of Art, the Museum of Modern Art and the Guggenheim Museum.

Sheldon Goldthwait Sr. bought the fully furnished cottage in December 1953. Furnishings included wooden painted cottage furniture, wicker porch furniture and some valuable antique Asian ceramics, etchings and paintings, including a Philadelphia card table by Querville. The Gallatin family removed some personal items, a couple of Walter Gay interior watercolors and two upholstered chairs. John Goldthwait still has an inventory of Gallatin's possessions prepared by George Goodrich, and the family kept many of the Gallatin items.

The house became the primary residence for the Goldthwait family, and they made a few changes to the property, including adding insulated storm windows and doors, updated plumbing for year-round use with "winter water" and forced hot water heat throughout the house except the storage rooms. They also expanded the cellar and added a bay window in the living room to replace two narrow windows that made the room very dark. Goldthwait and his wife raised their two sons, Sheldon Jr. and John, in the house. They renumbered and repainted the Gallatin sundial.

Sheldon Goldthwait served for seventeen years as president of the Bar Harbor Bank & Trust and was active in many local civic societies. He died in June 1965 at the age of sixty. After Goldthwait's death, his widow, Ruth S. Goldthwait, and family continued to live at the cottage on Mount Desert Street until they sold the property to Edward and Margaret Alley Douglas in 1992, four years before Mrs. Goldthwait's death. The Douglas family transformed the property into a bed-and-breakfast with many renovations and changed the name of the cottage to the Stone Throw Cottage Inn. Bob Collier bought the cottage in 2008 and sold it to the Heist family on June 30, 2013. In 2019, Peter Hastings bought the venerable cottage.

Holbrook House, built by Nathan Ash in 1879 at 74 Mount Desert Street. *Courtesy of the author.*

The debate over the oldest cottage on Mount Desert Street is complicated. Technically, the Stone Throw Cottage Inn should win since the building on the site goes back to the 1850s; however, the 1880s renovation retained the footprint but changed just about everything that had been in the Oliver Higgins cottage. The Mira Monte, on the other hand, was not built in 1868 and was most likely completed in its current form in 1880. The current Mira Monte should be dated at 1880 and the Stone Throw Cottage Inn at 1888 (if we include the tower). In conclusion, perhaps the winner is the Holbrook House at 74 Mount Desert Street (1879) or the Primrose Inn at 73 Mount Desert Street (1878), which were both built before the Mira Monte or the Stone Throw Cottage Inn renovation.[99]

Chapter 13

THE LOST GIRL OF HOLLAND AVENUE

JANE PARKER HOUSE
48 HOLLAND AVENUE

Mental health issues are not a new problem for Maine or the United States. Poor health, high fevers, bad diet and stress caused quite a bit of mental health issues in the late 1800s and early 1900s. Syphilis was common, and people who developed mental problems in the later stages of the disease were also grouped with those with mental illness. Epilepsy was considered a mental illness and treated with institutionalization. Chronic alcoholism often caused male family members to be committed to asylums for short or long stays, depending on the stage of addiction. The treatment for mental disorders during this era was institutionalization, with little or no medicines available to stabilize people. These illnesses usually resulted in ruined lives and economic hardship. Men were also committed for spousal abuse, and sometimes husbands committed their wives to get them out of their lives.

A Centralmaine.com article in 2012 provided the following information about the history of the Maine Insane Hospital in Augusta (later called the Augusta Mental Health Institute, AMHI):

> *When the Maine Insane Hospital opened in 1840, one of the first eight patients was a 24-year-old Augusta man who had been kept in handcuffs at the local poor house for several weeks, according to a 1965 history of the hospital. Another of the first patients was a 49-year-old Kittery woman who had expressed erroneous views on religion and who, it was thought, contracted her illness while caring for her mentally ill father and brother.*

48 Holland Avenue (stop no. 13), former home of Jane Parker, taken in the early 2000s before renovations. *Courtesy of the author.*

> *Early diagnoses often focused on socially unacceptable behavior, according to the cemetery project's report. Well into the 20th century, people were admitted to AMHI for conditions ranging from epilepsy to Alzheimer's disease. As a result, the list of 11,647 patients who died at AMHI includes people who didn't have mental illness, according to the cemetery project's report.*[100]

In 1881, there were 452 patients at the insane hospital, and the hospital was so crowded that 12 persons were refused admittance.[101]

Holland Avenue has a history of sad stories concerning mental illness. The man who the avenue was named for, Colonel William F. Holland from Savannah, Georgia, experienced severe health issues and pain during the last months of his life. He built the Primrose Inn (73 Mount Desert Street, 1878) and the Elmhurst Inn (formerly Graywood and Graycote, 40 Holland Avenue, 1880–81). Holland may have had a predisposition for depression since he was described as "never of a particularly cheery disposition."[102] Due to his depression, he attempted suicide once by trying to explode a gun carriage by his temple at the Hamilton Hotel on School Street. After recovering and vowing to hotel proprietor George W. Hamilton that he would never attempt suicide again, he received a Smith and Wesson five-

Arthur Ells, storekeeper and owner of the Ells Cottage, who was committed to the Maine Insane Hospital in Augusta due to his epilepsy. *Courtesy of the author.*

chambered revolver with ammunition through the mail from a Portland friend a few weeks later and killed himself on March 20, 1885, in his hotel room.

Arthur William Ells, who owned the Ells Cottage on Holland Avenue, suffered from severe epilepsy his whole life. In May 1889, the ailment became so debilitating that he was committed to the Maine Insane Hospital in Augusta by his wife, Julia, and his sister-in-law Almira Ash was appointed guardian. He was carried into the hospital in a catatonic state and was fed through his nose until a few weeks later, when he recovered and was released in August. Business stress and family matters caused him to relapse a few weeks later, and he threatened to kill family members. He was readmitted and then after a few months was released and never admitted to the hospital again. While at the hospital, and possibly on other occasions, he took bromides to control the epilepsy, which may have contributed to his death by kidney disease at the age of forty-eight ten years later.

Jane Parker was another person from Holland Avenue who experienced mental illness during her lifetime. Her grandmother Almira Ash shocked the town in 1860 when she openly raised her illegitimate daughter Minnie in a female-run household. Another child was born to the family on June 29, 1884, who was recorded as the second child of Almira but most likely was Minnie's child, born while she stayed with a relative, Mrs. Louisa Cloutman, in Dayton, Maine. This out-of-town birth might have been a way for Almira to help twenty-four-year-old Minnie escape the social stain of being the mother to an illegitimate child. The fact that the certificate says the father was Benjamin Ash of Eden (Bar Harbor), who had been dead for two years, and the mother was forty-four-year-old Almira leads one to believe the birth certificate was fraudulent. The child born in 1884 was Ellen "Nellie" Ash. Nellie came to live in Bar Harbor after Cloutman died in 1895, living as a lodger in the Harry C. Beswick household on Wescott Street in 1900 at the age of fifteen not far from the Julia Ells household, which was another Ash-subsidized household established after Arthur Ells's death. Nellie later lived with Almira Ash next door to Minnie.

Former home of Almira Ash, built in 1883, now part of the Mira Monte Inn. *Courtesy of the author.*

Perhaps due to Almira's plan, Minnie was able to marry Isaac E. Parker twelve years later on October 12, 1896, at Almira's house at 50 Holland Avenue. Minnie and Isaac had their first child, Jane Wheeler Parker, on February 3, 1898. A year and three months later, the couple had a second child, Maria Parker, who was prematurely born on June 21, 1899, and died four days later. Their third child, Isaac Parker Jr. (aka John), was born in 1901.

At some point before or after their marriage, either Minnie or Isaac contracted syphilis, which was later spread to the uninfected partner, leaving them both ill with the disease. Neither of the Parkers died of the illness; however, Isaac went insane during the last months of his life, and Minnie died of tuberculous. After Jane developed her mental issues, people felt her parents' illness was the cause of her problems. They also suspected that the premature death of the second child, Maria, might be related to the illness; however, John, the third child, was healthy with no known medical or mental issues.

Jane lived a healthy childhood with her parents on Holland Avenue. In September 1905, she started school in Bar Harbor at the age of seven and was popular, according to the newspaper accounts. An article in the newspaper about her birthday in February 1906 stated, "Little Jane W. Parker, daughter of Mr. and Mrs. Isaac Parker entertained 50 of her friends in honor of her

8th birthday with delicious refreshments."[103] In April of that year, "Little Miss Jane Parker entertained her friends on Saturday afternoon."[104] In November 1907, Jane attended a Halloween party at a Sunday school teacher's house from St. Saviour's Episcopal Church. Jane's school attendance was excellent during these early years, and she was an excellent student who loved to sit home reading books.

Isaac and Minnie Parker at some point were not able to provide a stable home for their two children, which was odd since both parents were active in the community and newspapers chronicled their civic and social life. The problem may have been with Minnie since the home life in this era was governed by the mother or wife. Minnie suffered from syphilis and TB, which may have affected her ability to provide care for her children.

Minnie's uncle Nathan Ash and his wife, Sarah, became active in the life of John, who became a surrogate son for the childless couple. They lived a few houses away on Spring Street. John enjoyed working with Nathan on his farm in Trenton and at his stable in Bar Harbor.

At some point, Jane went to live with her maternal aunt Adeline Higgins and her husband, Edwin. There was precedent for the couple helping family members in need. Fifteen years earlier, the couple had adopted Mabel Ells when her family had problems in the 1890s. Another aunt, Mariam Roberts, motored to the Jordan Pond house with her for tea and played bridge with her often. Although the family had come to her assistance, Jane felt that she was not given freedom and was nagged by her aunts and uncles. Her relatives' ages might have also been a factor in Jane's unhappiness, since all of her aunts and uncles were elderly.

Jane was bright but quiet in school. She was said to be normal, sensitive and reclusive. She graduated near the top of her class in 1916; however, the most popular girl contest printed in the newspaper that year showed that she was not popular, with only 18 votes compared to Ruth Stafford's 5,955 votes. The comments written about her in the December 1915 yearbook *Islander* include a strange poem written by editor Barbra A. Joy. The roasting of classmates by yearbook editors was common during this era, and Jane was not the only one to receive negative comments in the book. Unlike the other students who had paragraphs describing aspects of their personality, Jane's section only had a cryptic poem with Jane's full name amended with a middle name of "Blaine," which might have been an inside joke about her being connected to one of Maine's most famous politicians, James Blaine. The poem was:

JANE WHEELER BLAINE PARKER

Gentle Jane!
Heart in twain!
Who's the swain?
Life's a dream
Of things not seen,
Of fairy queen.
Nose in air,
Don't despair!
Have a care![105]

During the 1910s, Jane's activities seemed normal. She was active as historian for the YWCA, performed readings at Girls Friendly Society and was active with St. Saviour's Episcopal Church. In June 1916, as a member of the Bar Harbor High School class of 1916, her essay about Acadia was printed in the *Bar Harbor Times*. The well-written essay displayed Jane's strong intellect and writing skills. In May 1917, Jane was the representative for the Girls Friendly Society at the annual convention in Portland, Maine.

After graduation, Jane did not have a job or expand her education but remained active in civic and church organizations. In 1919, she had her first episode of manic depression (bipolar disorder) and was committed to the Eastern Maine Insane Hospital (later called the Bangor State Hospital and the Dorothea Dix Psychiatric Center) in Bangor by her aunt Adeline Higgins. One account said the episode began at the Casino, but this could not be confirmed.

The Eastern Maine Insane Hospital opened in July 1901 to provide space for people with mental disorders from Penobscot, Hancock, Washington, Aroostook and Piscataquis Counties. Between 1907 and 1910, the hospital underwent many expansions, including adding two additional wings to house male and female patients. All other patients from different regions of Maine were sent to the Maine Insane Hospital in Augusta. The capacity of the Bangor hospital was rated at 600; however, on January 21, 1920, there was a total of 684 patients: 355 men and 329 women.[106]

Jane had three mental hospitalizations from 1919 to 1925 for manic symptoms. Each of these confinements ranged from four to eight months, with at least a year between each visit. Her mental disorder improved after four months during her first hospitalization, and then she was stable for three years before the next hospitalization. The next confinement lasted eight months beginning in April 1922, with a release in January 1923. She then went a year and three months before her final hospitalization of the 1920s in March 1924, which lasted for nearly seven months. Jane was released in October 1925 and went nearly six years before her next hospitalization in April 1931.

A series of deaths in the 1920s may have contributed to the decline of Jane mentally. Her mother died while she was in her second hospitalization, and she did not attend the funeral. Her father, Isaac Parker, died of kidney trouble at the age of fifty-two during her third hospitalization. Her grandmother Almira Ash died in 1925, also while she was away.

This was an era when treatments for mental ailments included shock therapy, which they called "radiant heat, ultra violet, diathermy, sine wave (for women), galvanism and faradism, and electric needle," and cold and hot baths (hydrotherapy as sedatives).[107] After each of the seven stays during the 1920s and 1930s, Jane returned to Bar Harbor and lived in an apartment in the house her family owned at 48 Holland Avenue. John B. Ells and John Ash were appointed her guardians/trustees, with Ash dropping out after a few years. She had a financial trust from Mariam Roberts, the widow of the wealthy William Roberts, who owned the Newport House, which paid for her care for the rest of her life.

Jane had four hospitalizations in the 1930s. After a short stay of two months and two days from April to June 1931 for depression, she relapsed in October with a manic attack and stayed for the next fifteen months until July 16, 1933. In late December 1933, she attended a high school reunion group called the 1915 Sewing Club. During her time out of the hospital in 1934, her aunts Mariam and Adeline died. This must have been a huge loss for Jane since they helped raise her and the trio played bridge together for several years at Mariam's house, the Cadillac Cottage on Main Street, even though Adeline was nearly blind and Mariam shook from some disorder. Jane improved and was healthy for nearly two years until her hospitalization on June 14, 1935, with a depression that lasted twelve months until June 13, 1936. Two and a half years later was the start of her final hospitalization on December 29, 1938, for a manic episode.

Although family tradition stated that "poor Jane" contracted congenital syphilis from her mother, the 1938 examination during her last entry into the hospital confirmed there was no history or evidence of syphilis or gonorrhea in Jane. Instead, her condition was diagnosed as manic depression psychosis, and her mental issues may have been brought on by her family turmoil due to her parents' illness, difficult childhood or just inherited mood disorder.

Jane's treatment at the hospital did not improve her condition, and she did not return to Bar Harbor. She spent the next thirty-one years living in the Bangor hospital. During the 1960s, her doctors gave her Librium, which stabilized her condition, and in 1969, she was able to live in a halfway house in Ellsworth. She died there of artery disease and a cerebral hemorrhage a year later in 1970.

Her brother Isaac "John" Jr. graduated from Bar Harbor High School and Bryant and Stratton Business College in Boston. For over twenty-five years, he worked for the Somes House in Somesville and was manager from 1945 until his death in 1954. During the off-season, he was on the staff of several Florida hotels, including the Colony at Delray Beach, where he was employed during the 1953–54 season. Parker was chief of the Somesville Fire Company for four years and was chief during the Fire of 1947.

Nellie Ash Leonard, Jane's half-sister, and her husband, Clarence, established Leonard's Motel (later called the Aurora Motel) on the corner of Holland Avenue and Mount Desert Street on the Goodrich Shop lot. At this spot, the Fire of 1947 came closest to destroying the town. Nellie, a distinguished-looking woman with white hair, had a wonderful personality and was loved by the local community and the tourists who stayed at her motel. She wore a beautiful ruby ring that her aunt Mariam Roberts gave her and was remembered for her loud call down Holland Avenue to her husband at mealtime while he talked to friends at the Bar Harbor Motor Company on Cottage Street (now the Hannaford Supermarket, 86 Cottage Street): "Clarence, you et yet?" Nellie passed in 1957 and is buried at Ledgelawn Cemetery along with the rest of the family.

Other Holland Avenue Sites: 41 Holland Avenue (1900); Castlemaine Inn (39 Holland Avenue, 1885); Newman Cottage/Holland Inn (35 Holland Avenue, 1895); and the Crossways (4 Holland Avenue, 1901).

Chapter 14

THE MISSING BLOCK

WALTER BIRD HOUSE
10 HOLLAND AVENUE

During the last three years of his life, Captain Benjamin Ash developed a piece of his property at the corner of Cottage Street and Holland Avenue that was known as the Ash Block for many years. A map of Eden (Bar Harbor) from 1880 shows the corner of Cottage Street and Holland Avenue filled with trees and no houses; however, by the next map of the area in 1881, buildings are shown on the property, including a house for Ash; his eldest son, Alonzo; his grandson Israel Ash; and a rental house labeled with the name C.F. Seammons but called the Preble house by the Ash family. These properties were located on the land to the left of the Bar Harbor Municipal Building (former Bar Harbor High School) (93 Cottage Street, 1907), which today is occupied by the Irving Oil Gas Station, a parking lot, rental properties and a private residence. Debbie Dyer from the Bar Harbor Historical Society does not believe that any of the buildings currently on this site were part of this original Ash development. The Alonzo Ash house that was located closest to the old high school was torn down to expand the Irving parking lot several years ago, and another building on the property being used as an apartment burned recently and was razed.

The seeds for this development of the block began in 1877 when sixty-eight-year-old Maria (Mariah) Ash divorced her sixty-two-year-old husband a year after Captain Ash threw her out of their Holland Avenue house and moved forty-six-year-old Eliza Ann Crabtree, the widow of Hancock Point captain Reuben Crabtree, in to live with him. Mrs. Ash sued Captain Ash for $1,000 ($24,209.71) but received cutting and hauling of wood, use of his

10 Holland Avenue (stop no. 14), the former residence of Walter and Loretta Bird that replaced the Preble house (aka Charles F. Seammons house) in the Ash Block in 1905. *Courtesy of the author.*

cow and shed with lumber in the divorce settlement.[108] Real estate and other local records suggest that Captain Ash provided a house next to the Ells Cottage on Holland Avenue for his wife to live in after the divorce settlement that today is 48 Holland Avenue.

This divorce must have caused a local scandal, and six months after it was granted, the Ashes reconciled and remarried in January 1878. Pressure from Ash's eight children; his wife's family, the Higginses; and other locals must have had an influence on their remarriage. Eliza Ann Crabtree left town and married fifty-eight-year-old John D. Blaisdell from West Sullivan in 1879. This marriage was troubled; Blaisdell posted a notice in the *Ellsworth American* in 1892 indicating that his wife, Eliza, had fled his bed and board. She must have returned, since her *Ellsworth American* obituary on July 30, 1896, said she was the wife of Blaisdell and that she died of "a long, painful illness."

Although the divorce was nullified when the couple remarried, Captain Ash had the unique privilege of paying for attorneys for both sides of the divorce. The law firm representing Captain Ash in the divorce, Hale & Emery from Ellsworth, sent its bill to him on May 16, 1877, at the conclusion of the case. The firm was founded by Eugene Hale, a prominent Maine senator, and Lucilius Alonzo Emery, a future associate justice to the Maine Supreme Court. A year later, Captain Ash paid a six-dollar bill from his wife's divorce attorney, Andrew Peters Wiswell, who later became chief justice of the Maine Supreme Judicial Court on September 6, 1878.

Due to either financial difficulty or an effort to raise money for his new building projects, Captain Ash sold the right of way to Frenchman Bay (Holland Avenue) leading to Hamor's Wharf and other properties to Colonel Holland in 1877. Holland later built the Primrose and the Elmhurst on the two pieces of land he purchased. Reverend C.S. Leffingwell bought the Primrose and Elmhurst from Holland and upgraded the properties. Leffingwell built the Old Rectory (1880s) on Mount Desert Street between the Primrose and Mira Monte and the Clover Cottage (96 Cottage Street, 1880). Leffingwell also bought the Ells Cottage (44 Holland Avenue, 1876) and razed the building in the 1890s.

In his quest to build the new block, Captain Ash bought building materials from various Eden (Bar Harbor) merchants for his building projects. The purchases included white lead paint, paintbrushes and paper from Higgins Brothers Store, located between the Grand Central Hotel and Rodick House on Main Street, in October/November 1881. Nails, hinges, screws, rasps and butts came from Desisle and Brewer Store on June 16, 1881. Planks, boards and shingles were purchased from R. Hamor and Sons,

Mrs. Ash's receipt from R. Hamor & Sons Dry Goods in 1885. *Courtesy of the author.*

and J.E. Clark supplied hemlock and pine boards. Mrs. Ash completed the construction after her husband's death with her April 16, 1883 purchase of boards for finishing the inside of the house, clapboarding and shingling for the roof $32.50 ($809.96) from A.J. Bennett. The receipts for pine, spruce and hemlock boards, clip boards and shingle in the boards for finishing inside the house and clapboarding one side and shingling in the summer of 1880 were for the Ash houses from suppliers C.P. De Sailer and A.J. Bennett.

Captain Ash's health took a turn for the worse in January 1882, and he quickly completed his will on January 12, four days before his death on January 16. The will, which was very comprehensive, was witnessed by Dr. Rogers, Henry Higgins and James Knox. There was dissention in the family concerning the details of the will, which awarded most of Ash's $5,000 estate to his widow, Maria (Mariah) Ash, and three sons, Alonzo, Orlando and Nathan. Ash's four daughters and one granddaughter were given only Green Mountain woodlots, and his youngest daughter, Julia Ells, contested the will in August 1882, saying that Ash was not of sound mind when he wrote up the terms and that he had not signed it. Orlando Ash, who was appointed administrator in the will, declined the position in August 1881 after posting the required notices in the *Ellsworth American*, the Eden Post Office and R.F. Suminsby's store notifying people that Ash died and that they needed to submit any pending bills. Suminsby's store was located on Main Street in the Bunker Block opposite the Rodick House and provided

Former house of Alonzo Ash and the first building built in the Ash Block, which was razed in the early 2000s for the Irving parking lot. *Courtesy of the author.*

Walter and Loretta Bird playing piano with friends, early 1900s, at their house at 10 Holland Avenue. *Courtesy of the Bar Harbor Historical Society.*

"Foreign and American Dry Goods, Dress Goods and Ladies and gents furnishings."[109] Julia Ash withdrew her complaint when a promissory note she owed the estate was waived.

After Ash's grandson Israel Ash, who was a blacksmith, died suddenly of blood poisoning in August 1892 from an infected hand wound, his widow, Lauretta Ash, inherited most of the property on the Ash Block. White and Carpenter rebuilt the houses currently at 8 and 10 Holland Avenue in 1905 for Lauretta and her second husband, Captain Walter Bird. Their main residence might have replaced the house owned by C.F. Seammons in the 1880s maps (the Preble house). The other new building (10 Holland Avenue) had a lower story as a finished storehouse for W.C. Allison with second-floor tenement. The Birds moved into their new home in December 1905. This house survives today as the last remnant of this lost block.

Although Ash saw many changes to the town during his lifetime that improved the lifestyle of Bar Harbor residents, Captain Benjamin Ash did not live to see Bar Harbor's first electric lights installed in July 1884.

Chapter 15

THE MUSIC HALL, THE CASINO AND THE WAY BAK BALL

ALONZO ASH HOUSE
6 SUMMER STREET

As Eden developed into a prosperous town, the establishment of a music hall for musical performances, lectures and dancing became a priority. Large hotels such as the Rodick House and the Grand Central Hotel established music rooms to entertain their guests in the 1880s during the summer months. The problem was that none of these venues could be used in the off-season without heating. The only other available venue was the upper floor of the schoolhouse on School Street, which was considered inadequate. In late 1887, a group of six young local entrepreneurs led by W.H. Higgins built a one-story Music Hall on Main Street at the intersection of Wayman Lane. The building had a stove at either end to heat the building in the winter months, a stage on the western side of the building and a hardwood dance floor. The Music Hall quickly overshadowed the hotel music rooms during the summer months and dominated the entertainment in the winter months, consisting of lectures, theater, orchestras and dances. The hall opened on January 2, 1888, with a masquerade ball and was said to have been "a great boom to the town" during the winter months, including the Public Lecture Course, a series of ten lectures given by local talent that was very popular.[110]

The Music Hall was active and loved by the locals and summer community until an August 1893 fire consumed the building. A letter in the newspaper remarked about the sad loss in the fire of the iconic painting on the Music Hall's wall of the Cormac's Chapel at the Rock of Cashel

6 Summer Street (stop no. 15), the closest surviving building to the empty lot where the Casino once stood, was built by J.E. Clark in the 1880s and was the former site of Maggies and Fathom restaurants. *Courtesy of the author.*

in Tipperary, Ireland. There was controversy about the fire since the newly installed fire hydrants that were dependent on the new Bar Harbor Water Company had low pressure and the fire chief refused to provide a fire truck from the fire station.

In 1894, Charles E. Lindall, well-known solo cornetist from Boston and leader of Lindall's military band, built a new hall on the same piece of land on Main Street between Wayman Lane and Center Street. The hall, called the "New Music Hall," was built by carpenter Seth Hopkins, who later became one of the original Way Baks in the late 1890s. Lindall leased the building to George Joy and Ernest Mayo, who had their own orchestra. Today, the Havana Restaurant (318 Main Street, 1900) is located on this corner of Main Street and Wayman Lane. The restaurant was one of the older buildings that were moved when the Agamont Park was developed in the 1930s.

The first Hay Seeders Ball (Way Bak Ball) was thrown on Monday, February 25, 1895, at the Music Hall. The ball was a local response to being shut out of the elegant balls thrown by the summer colony. Instead, the townspeople threw their own ball in the off-season, poking fun at the way they were perceived as hicks by their rich patrons. No one could have imaged that the Way Bak Ball would outlive the summer colony that the gala poked fun at.

The *Bar Harbor Record* stated on February 27, 1895, that guests received invitations to the Hay Seeders Ball "written on brown paper, sprinkled with hay seed and enclosed in a yellow envelope."[111] At 7:30 p.m., the "melodious cow bell" rang, and Samanthy in a "sunbonnet and a calico gown" and Ike "attired a la mode of half a century ago, with long white hair and whiskers," led the grand march of about one hundred couples.[112] A written description of the dance order was made with crayons, and the hall was decorated with "sheaves, grains, pumpkin jacks, farm products and farming implements of every kind."[113] From stone jars, labeled Old Rye and Medford Rum, was served lemonade to drink with the molasses doughnuts and gingersnaps. The entertainers wore boutonnieres of ripe wheat. Monaghan's Orchestra played "the old-fashioned dances which were kept up till a late hour."[114]

The twenty-two hosts responsible for the invitations to the 1895 Hay Seeders Ball were Charles Allen, Alonzo Ash, E.N. Benson, A.G. Bulger, J.E. Clark, Frank Connors, John Connors, D.L. Drew, J.E. Foster, Charles Green, A.L. Higgins, B.S. Higgins, C.L. Higgins, S.N. Higgins, T.C. Higgins, E.C. Parker, Andrew Rodick, G.E. Rodick, S.H. Rodick, Nathan Salisbury, V.G. Wasgatt and B.E. Whitney. Although not listed as hosts, Frank Leighton and Fred A. Foster were the leaders of the march of one hundred couples dressed as Samanthy and Ike. Misses Bunker and Hodgkins were two of the female attendees.

The Music Hall was also popular for music, movies, dances and even roller skating from 1894 until it closed in 1926. It was an official voting space during the 1900 presidential election. Minstrel shows were also a big part of the Music Hall's events. In 1888, the Music Hall presented two showings in one night of the famous prohibition play *Ten Nights in a Bar Room* for ten and fifteen cents. Monaghan's Orchestra played there often.

The hall received major renovations at least twice, in 1907 and 1923, and the dance floor must have been of good quality, since Lindall claimed that his sales price for the hall of $600 in May 1925 would only cover the amount he paid for the dance floor.[115] The Music Hall was so popular and well known that Lindall never included an address for the various events advertised in the newspapers over at least three decades.

Another regular patron of the Music Hall was the Colored Folks Annual Dance, which was held twenty times at the Music Hall before it hosted its last dance there on May 25, 1925. This event was hosted by Hanley Mathews

Davis, an African American from Cambridge, Massachusetts, who traveled to Bar Harbor in the 1920s and worked as a shoeshiner. In the Cambridge area, Davis was a waiter for several years at the Hotel Ericson on Commonwealth Avenue, a chauffeur for a private family and a steward at the Collage Club. A year before their last dance in 1924, F. Eugene Farnsworth was scheduled to provide a lecture supporting the Ku Klux Klan on a Sunday afternoon at the Music Hall, but the lecture was moved to the larger Casino due to the high number of advance tickets sold.

A month before the first Hay Seeders Ball, a weird disclaimer appeared in the *Bar Harbor Record* stating that a party was advertised at the Hapworth & Burr Hall by the "Old Jolly Boys" for the following week, but the hosts listed on the bill—Osmond Emery, Edgar Trussell, Henry Bragdon and Arthur Partridge—disclaimed that they were the hosts. All of the men listed in this news item were founding members of the Way Baks in 1896 but were not included as hosts for the first Hay Seeders Ball in 1895. Did the "Old Jolly Boys" become the Way Baks and take over hosting the party in 1896?

During the next year, a core group of Way Baks came together, including Lionel E. (Ren) (Owen) Stewart, Osmond Emery, Edgar Trussell, Henry Bragdon, Arthur Partridge, William Jordan and others, to establish the group of hosts that successfully hosted the party for the next seventeen years. From 1901 to 1913, the fifteen Way Baks grew to the "famous 23" and included the following men during these years: P.W. Blanchfield, Henry Bragdon, Frank Brewer, Martin Clark, George Cleaves, Lon Cleaves, Osmond Emery, Charlie Fernald, Patsy Fitzgerald, P.D. Foster (Gilly), Mark Grant, T.C. Higgins, Will Higgins, Frank Holden, Seth Hopkins, Reg Ingalls, Fountain "Fount" Jellison, William R. "Bill" Jordan, Frank Leighton, Mel Milliken, Arthur Partridge, Horace Pettengill, Mark F. Richards, Captain Chas (Rooney) Shand, Charles Shea, Fred Small, G.E. Soper, Lionel E. (Ren) (Owen) Stewart, Leon Tabbutt, Edgar Trussell, Eben Whitaker and C.E. Whitmore.[116]

The next six Way Bak Balls, from 1896 to 1901, were held at the Hapworth & Burr Hall on Eden Street across the street from the current DeGregoire Green. Herbert E. Hapworth, known as Hep, was partnered with John H. Burr, a former mariner, in a successful cabinetmaking business that was located on the same property. The hall, which was built in the late 1880s, had one of the best dance floors in the county with a capacity for a least a couple hundred people but was not as big as the Music Hall. When the Music Hall burned down in 1893, all scheduled local dances were moved to the Hapworth & Burr Hall for the remainder

The Casino was the center of Bar Harbor activities from 1901 to 1970. *Courtesy of the author.*

of the season. After Hapworth's wife died suddenly in January 1900, Hep leased the building to Ernest Mayer, who established the West End Dance Hall, which was active under that name during the rest of the year. In 1901, the hall was used for one more Way Bak Ball before Mayer began his lease. This was apparently the swan song for the hall since it did not reopen as the West End Dance Hall in 1901 and the next Way Bak Ball was held at the Casino.

Because of the space limitations of existing town venues, a movement began in 1890 to build a major entertainment complex in the center of Bar Harbor for the locals and summer residents. The building was built in the summer of 1901 with a design from famous Mount Desert Island architect Milton Stratton, who is best known for his partnership with Fred Savage. The Casino quickly became the center of social activities for the island during the summer season, when eight thousand people lived in the area, and during the off-season with a resident population of two thousand.

The Way Bak Ball was the most consistent annual event held at the Casino during its sixty-nine years of existence. The hall was larger and better located in the center of town than either the Music Hall or Hapworth & Burr Hall. One of the active Way Baks in the early days, Osmond Emery, was the manager of the Casino for several years. The more socially connected

Building of the Arts (1907) was never considered to host this event due to its limited capacity of 380 seats and seasonal availability.

The Way Bak Ball was an invitation-only affair. The original Way Baks and, later, the forty Hay Seeders were responsible for selecting the invitees for the annual event, which was attended by several hundred people each year. The invitation was valued since the Way Bak committee had to place a notice in the *Bar Harbor Record* in 1901 reminding people that the event was "strictly private, not a public affair," and invitations were required for admittance at the door.[117] Lionel (Owen) Stewart said in the early years that they would not distribute the invitations until the morning of the dance.[118] The invitation reprinted in the *Bar Harbor Record* in 1911 used the unique Way Bak language to announce the ball:

> *Do yew no, we fellers, even if we air WAY BAK, does no sumpthin besides taters and punkins. We've gorn and gut the TOWN MEETIN HOUSE, which them hi-toned rusticaters like to call the KURSENO yew no, and thare we is goin to hev a BALL and it will be Munday nite Febry the twenty7th 1911 & BY COSH IT WILL BE A GOOD ONE.*[119]

Thomas Carol "T.C." Higgins was a consistent Way Bak host during the early decades of the ball. A March 8, 1911 *Bar Harbor Record* article said that Higgins always felt bad each year because he wanted to give an invitation to everyone. His father, Willard Higgins, ran the Exchange Hotel, and Thomas owned a grocery/dry goods store on Des Isle Avenue for many years. He was known for his cottage on Indian Point called "Uncle Tom's Cabin," which was mentioned often in newspaper items during the twentieth century. His Indian Point property continues to be owned by his descendants.

In 1914, a new group consisting of a "number of people styling themselves as hay seeders" threw a Way Bak Ball on February 24, 1914.[120] Their invitation was in the usual Way Bak language and offered the ball as a way to forget about the twenty-three months of "automobile agitation" since cars had been allowed on the island.[121] A year later, the new organization, the 40 Hayseeders, threw their first official ball on February 1, 1915, rebranding the dance with its original name, the Hayseeders Ball (aka Hay Seeders Ball). They were called Hayseeders rather than Way Baks (aka Way Bak fellas). The larger number of hosts helped offset the cost of the ball and provided enough hosts to ensure a well-attended dance each year. Newspaper accounts recorded the number of attendees at various balls as between five hundred and eight hundred people at the Casino, which was much larger than the earlier balls. This new group consisted of old-timers and new younger people such as Archie Getchell, who was the master of ceremonies at the Hayseeders luncheon at the New Florence Hotel (new name for the Hotel Porcupine on Main Street, 1887) in February 1915, three years before the fire that consumed the hotel. A newspaper story in 1917 stated that "the Hayseeders are successors to the famous Way Bak organization, and the ball will be conducted on much the same lines."[122]

Although the Famous 23 changed over the years to the 40 Hayseeders, one constant participant for many years was Lionel Stewart, who attended the Way Bak Ball in 1958 when he was ninety-one. It was his sixty-fourth Way Bak Ball. His wife, Violet, who was seventeen years younger than Lionel, also attended. They were married for fifty-two years, and it is not known if they attended the next two balls before his death in 1961 and her passing a year later.

News items during the 1940s and 1950s often included the names of out-of-town people who attended the ball and the parties that went on before, during the intermission and after the ball. These parties became a huge part of the ball events each year. Balls were eventually moved to weekends rather than during the week, which ensured better participation and allowed out-of-town guests to participate in the dance and the parties.

One of the traditions that has always been key to the opening of the event is the grand march. Couples followed the leaders of the march while onlookers in the balcony of the Casino watched. Newspaper accounts reported that the grand march was led over the years by various people, including Frank Leighton and Fred Foster (1895), Edgar and Mrs. Trussell (1902), Lorenzo and Mrs. Stewart (1907), Eben and Mrs. Whitaker (1908), Orlando Ash and Miss Maude Blanchfield (1923–28), Mr. and Mrs. George Beard (1932) and Mrs. and Mrs. Roger Cunningham (1966).

Other Way Bak Balls and Hayseeder Balls were held in other Mount Desert Island towns such as Hulls Cove, Northeast Harbor, Salisbury Cove, Seal Harbor, Somesville and Town Hill. There was a Junior Hayseeders Ball also held at the Casino for several years and a Way Bak skating party thrown at the Rainbow Roller Rink in 1941. Even Dan Herlihy and the Dreamwood got in the act with a Way Bak Ball thrown in November 1927, with eighty-four-year-old Orlando Ash and Mrs. Shirley Joyce heading up the grand march. All of these events gave local people something to look forward to during the cold months of the year. The other balls held on Mount Desert Island kept the original name of Way Bak Ball rather than Hayseeders Ball.

Way Bak Ball during the 1940s at the Casino. *Courtesy of the author.*

The Casino was also used for other community events over the years, including boxing matches, World War II VE Day and VJ Day celebrations, municipal elections and council meetings. One very memorable event was the 1955 basketball tournament when the Bar Harbor Sea Siders went on to be state basketball champions, winning many of their exciting games at the Casino.[123] In the late 1950s, the team was forced to stop playing basketball at the Casino and went to play in Northeast Harbor because the Casino was designated not a regulation court due to the tightening of rules.

During the 1960s, the building continued to be used by grammar school basketball teams and the high school for gym classes and assemblies. Other events such as Baccalaureates, May Day card parties, Class Days and dances with bands continued to be held at the Casino during the 1960s.

The last straw for the building was the new regionalized high school, built in 1968. After the new building was completed, the old building lost its purpose as a gym and became a costly white elephant to maintain. The building was razed in May 1970 by Charles Arnold, who commented at the time that it was a very difficult building to raze due to the solid construction.[124] Today, the only reminder of the footprint of this venerable building is the parking lot of 6 Summer Street on the corner of Cottage and Bridge Streets. After the Casino's demise, the Hayseeders (Way Bak) Balls were hosted at the

A History Lover's Guide to Bar Harbor

The Casino during the 1960s. *Courtesy of the Bar Harbor Historical Society.*

Masonic Hall (18 High Street, 1888) and the Atlantic Oceanside Hotel & Event Center. The Masonic Hall was the former Bar Harbor grammar and high school and was built before the first Hayseeders Ball was held.

Although the Way Bak/Hayseeders Ball is a loved and respected Bar Harbor institution, in 1895, another ball in February was considered the "event of the season" and far more important than the first Hayseeders Ball at the time.[125] This "brilliant ball" was held by twenty-three ladies with three hundred guests at the Music Hall. Unlike the Hayseeders Ball, this ball was all about elegance. The costumes were the "prettiest ever seen in Bar Harbor," with "nearly every lady dancer" wearing "a white or delicately tinted gown making a pleasing effect."[126] Pullen's Orchestra from Bangor played "the most entrancing music and in truth joy was unconfined."[127] If only these ladies could have continued their ball each year, Bar Harbor would have had a difficult time determining which ball was truly the event of the winter season.

6 Summer Street: The house next to the Casino lot was the site in March 1919 of a complaint by Charles Fowler against eighty-year-old "prominent local socialist" Alonzo Ash for chopping and splitting wood between 12:30 and 1:30 a.m.[128] Judge Connors did not accept Ash's explanation that he was not able to keep the fires burning enough to keep his house warm. He charged him $5.34 with the assurance that Ash would not do it again.

Family gatherings must have been interesting at this time since Alonzo's brother Orlando listed his profession on census records as "capitalist." The two brothers were business partners in the early 1870s with the Ash Brothers Eden House near the Atlantic House (later called the Louisburg and the Lorraine Hotel). While running the hotel, Alonzo Ash lost a court case to the Douglas family because of his sheep roaming on their Atlantic House property. Leon Hubbard said that when he was a boy, Alonzo's daughter Everlena cleaned out the Summer Street house and threw Civil War uniforms and dozens of glass negatives in the trash. Sadly, Leon and his friends were not able to retrieve any of these treasures before they were carted away.

Chapter 16

WORLD WAR I AND THE SPANISH INFLUENZA

GEORGE EDWIN KIRK AMERICAN LEGION POST 0025
70 COTTAGE STREET

The Spanish influenza of 1918 had a huge impact on Bar Harbor, as it did most towns in America. World War I had already completely disrupted the normal patterns of life in the town, with young men being drafted or enlisted into military service and traveling to Boston and other locations to join the fight in Europe. Just as the Americans and their allies were preparing for the big Hundred Days Offensive, the influenza hit like a tidal wave.

The influenza pandemic of 1918 had three phases. The first started in March in Kansas near Camp Funston and ended around June after troops coming from America infected Europe. Spain became the first place to report on the sickness during the first phase, since it was neutral during the war and had no wartime censorship. Thus, the deadly disease was given the name Spanish influenza even though it most likely originated in Haskell County, Kansas.

In the summer of 1918, the virus mutated in Europe and came back to the United States via ship. The location for this arrival was Commonwealth Pier in Boston in August 1918. At that time, a simultaneous epidemic occurred in Brest, France, and Freetown, Sierra Leone. After a few weeks, the disease made its way to Camp Devens in Ayer, Massachusetts.

The 1918 Spanish influenza killed its victims with two punches. The first viral punch weakened the immune system, and then the person contracted pneumonia, either lobar or broncho, which killed them. This influenza was unusual from other strains because many of those who died

70 Cottage Street (stop no. 16), George Edwin Kirk American Legion Post 0025. *Courtesy of the author.*

were between the ages of twenty and forty, in the prime of their lives. The influenza caused an extensive overreaction to the virus in this youthful group, which caused bleeding and extensive damage to internal organs. There was also a great risk of contracting meningitis and tuberculous after recovering from the disease due to the weakened physical condition. Pregnant women were extremely vulnerable to death from influenza, and babies born from an ill mother had a shorter lifespan than those born to mothers who were not infected.

Camp Devens was considered ground zero for the first major outbreak of the second phase in the United States, which would be the deadliest. Dr. Welsh from Johns Hopkins University (which was the closest thing to the CDC at that time) visited Camp Devens to observe the illness firsthand. After he saw the chest of a soldier opened at the camp and observed the "blue swollen lungs" with "wet, foamy surfaces," he remarked, "This must be some new kind of infection or plague."[129] He left the camp, came down with the disease and fortunately recovered in a few weeks to continue his quest to identify and stop the deadly contagion.

On September 28, 1918, the *Bar Harbor Times* first mentioned the illness that was plaguing the military bases all over the country. The delay in this reporting may have been related to war censorship; however, as the disease spread to the civilian population, it became difficult to contain the story. By late September, the War Department had to suspend the draft due to the camp epidemic nationwide.

The September 28 newspaper notice in the *Bar Harbor Times* provided positive news about the condition of four local soldiers who enlisted at different times. The four soldiers—Tobias L. Roberts, Morris Franklin, Maurice Sopey and Dr. John B. Ells—illustrated the extent of the epidemic, since they had all gotten sick around the same time in different locations. There is limited information in the newspaper sources about the details of the illness experienced by Franklin, Sopey or Roberts; however, the John B. Ells influenza story was a family tale that was often repeated by his daughter.

Ells had been on active reserve for a year, since the fall of 1917, when he finally was called up to duty on September 1, 1918, and traveled to Camp Devens, where he was in the Dental Corps, which was his profession. During the second week at Devens, he caught the influenza and became very ill. He was brought to the infirmary of the camp, where two soldiers from Maine were recovering from the disease and were saddened to see the serious condition of Dr. Ells. Feeling that he was doomed to die, they flipped a coin to see who would accompany the body to Bar Harbor when he passed. After a lengthy stay in the hospital with several crises, Dr. Ells recovered. He later learned that the two men who flipped the coin relapsed and died. Relapse was common since the best recovery required an extended stay in bed, which was hard for young soldiers to follow. The nurse who took care of Ells during his illness also succumbed to the disease.

Tobias Roberts served at the District Enrolling Office in Boston from May 15, 1917, to October 28, 1918. This location put him in a potentially dangerous place when the virus first came to Boston in August. He returned to the job after he recovered and his immunity to the disease protected him from further illness.

Morris E. Franklin was at sea when he got sick. He eventually went to the Newport, Rhode Island port, where he received treatment. Other local people who came down with the illness at sea also went to Newport, which was one of the locations for treatment for sailors. Max Franklin, owner of a Main Street dry goods store, traveled to be with his son.

Maurice B. Soper may also have been at Camp Devens or another camp when he got sick. Soper enrolled in the USNRF (navy) at Bar Harbor on April 4, 1917, for 236 days and then was discharged at the Navy Yard in

Boston on November 27, 1917. He enlisted again in AEF (army) at Ellsworth on June 22, 1918, as a private. He was a member of the 151st Dep Brigade at Devens until August 3, 1918, and then a member of Company F, 73rd Infantry, until he was honorably discharged on January 29, 1919. Soper's father, George E. Soper, was a successful Cottage Street butcher/grocer. All four of these sick Bar Harbor residents were said to have been in "camp hospitals" when they were ill.

Military furlough of troops became the most common means of civilian transmission of the virus. Looking at the *Bar Harbor Times* in the weeks before the disease became a pandemic, weekly news items reported about local boys returning home on furlough from Camp Devens and other locations. Furloughs were common during the month of September before being halted in October during the worst days of the pandemic. Unhealthy soldiers from these camps came home to visit Bar Harbor and other towns, spreading the disease throughout the United States. Some relatives of men sick at Camp Devens from Maine came to the camp to visit, which also helped the virus spread to the state.

Various news stories from the fall of 1918 noted that the local girls heeded the call to help. They include eighteen-year-old Marjorie Milliken, who came to the State House at Boston. She trained as a "pupil nurse at the Boston State Hospital." She had two brothers in the AEF: Allan in France and Paul at Camp Devens. Agnes Campbell and Esther West from Bar Harbor "responded to the recent urgent call for nurses sent out from the State Board of Health," working in Kittery.[130] Another story noted that Kathleen Morris, Beulah Paine and Mrs. Harry Copp from Bar Harbor went to Lisbon Falls for "intensive training in influenza nursing."

Dr. C.C. Morrison was one of the prominent doctors in Bar Harbor during this era. He had an established practice dating back to the late 1800s, with an office on Cottage Street. Morrison was instrumental in the establishment and success of the Mount Desert Island Hospital and was helping with the treatment of the influenza victims until his daughter, who was living in Washington, D.C., was stricken with a serious case of the disease. The town took notice when Morrison traveled to the nation's capital to assist in her recovery. Her story fortunately had a happy ending with full recovery.

Among the 260 members of the army, navy and naval reserve from Bar Harbor during World War I, 10 were listed as not surviving the conflict. All of these 10 people appear to have died from influenza-related illness except Roland Leland, who was missing in action on October 14, 1918, but not confirmed dead until a year later after his family was notified that his body was interred in a cemetery in France. Cecil H. Hodson was an engineer who served in France at Saint-Mihiel and later died of influenza in February 1919. Frederick J. Barstow died of the disease at Knox County General Hospital in Rockland on October 15, 1918, after serving in the navy for four months on USS *Cherokee* SP 1104. Harold Eugene Dow died of influenza on November 29, 1918, after serving in the navy at Section Headquarters in Bar Harbor.

The American Legion Post in in Bar Harbor (70 Cottage Street, 1919) was named for George Kirk in 1919. He achieved fame in the war through his heroics at the Battles of Chateau-Thierry, St. Mihiel and Meuse-Argonne. Kirk ended up dying on November 20, 1918, from pneumonia caused by influenza.

Red Cross nurse Frances Donovan left Bar Harbor for Camp Dix, New Jersey, on September 16, 1918. She died at the camp hospital on September 30 of pneumonia and was given full military honors at her funeral on October 2 in Bar Harbor.[131] She was the only woman who served during World War I from Bar Harbor to be included on the list of war dead for the town.

Odd Fellows Hall (39 Cottage Street, 1915) was converted into an emergency hospital in October 1918 to handle the overflow from Mount Desert Hospital (8 Wayman Lane, 1898). Mrs. Fred Higgins, a trained nurse, managed the local housewives who took care of the patients in the thirty-seven-bed facility. Most of the patients came from the naval reserve radio station in Otter Creek.

On November 23, Leverett D. Bristol, Maine state commissioner of health and chairman of the State Emergency Influenza Committee, stated that 25,863 cases of influenza and 457 deaths were reported to the State Department of Health from various local boards of health throughout the state. The final Maine tally reached 47,000 people sick with 5,000 deaths in a population of 760,000. One-half of the 5,000 perished in October 1918. The leading associated causes of death with the Spanish influenza were pneumonia, pregnancy, tuberculosis and heart disease. About 50 percent of those who died were between twenty and forty years old, which was very unusual for influenza. As a comparison, Camp Devens, with a population of 45,000, had at least 14,000 cases and 751 deaths by the end of September 1918 from the Spanish influenza.

The annual report for 1918 reported that Bar Harbor had 491 influenza cases in October and November 1918 and 30 deaths from pneumonia

John B. Ells and other Bar Harbor soldiers at Fort Devens, Massachusetts, 1918. *Courtesy of the author.*

following the disease. This cause of death was six times the next cause, which was cancer. It also stated in the report that many other influenza cases were not reported. In early 1919, another 107 cases were reported in the Town Hill area. The population of Bar Harbor was 3,622 in 1920.

In 1918, Bar Harbor had two pest houses owned by the town; these were later called isolation hospitals. One was at Eagle Lake valued at $500. The second one was located at Eagle Lake Road and Woodbury Road near Kebo Golf Course and was valued at $9,000. The Eagle Lake property was supplied by Frank Brewer when he acquired the old pest house property on Corkscrew Hill Road near Witch Hole Pond from the town in 1904. The Eagle Lake facility was used until 1927, when it was sold to George Dorr. The Woodbury facility, located near the intersection of Woodbury Road and Eagle Lake Road, was designed by Fred Savage and completed after 1913. This location, also called the contagious hospital, was closed in the 1940s and burned in the 1947 fire.

Over 675,000 Americans and between 50 and 100 million people worldwide died during the Spanish influenza pandemic of 1918 and 1919. India lost between 10 and 20 million people to the disease. More U.S. soldiers died from influenza than from combat wounds in the war.

John Ash with a soldier in France, 1918. *Courtesy of the author.*

Noting that only 20 percent of those who became ill ultimately died from the disease shows the enormous impact that the Spanish influenza had on the people living at that time. Another one hundred years passed before the United States and Bar Harbor experienced a pandemic as serious as the Spanish influenza of 1918.

Other Cottage Street Sites: Epicurean Epi's Pizza (8 Cottage Street, 1897); Village Emporium (14 Cottage Street, 1889); Cadillac North Face (23 Cottage Street, 1900); Cadillac AG (29 Cottage Street, 1910); Bulgers/Rosalies (46 Cottage Street, 1900); "59 Cottage Street" (59 Cottage Street, 1870); Briarfield/Central House (60 Cottage Street, 1887); Dr. Norton's office/MDI Dental Arts (67 Cottage Street, 1887); Robert Hodgkins's residence/A4 Architects (69 Cottage Street, 1900); H.A. Brown Furniture/Salon NaturELLES (74 Cottage Street, 1900); Jordan's Restaurant (80 Cottage Street, 1890); Quimby House Inn and Spa (109 Cottage Street, 1900); Everett Liscombe residence/Coplon Assoc./Dobbs Prod. (112 Cottage Street, 1900); and Haraden residence/2 Cats Restaurant (130 Cottage Street, 1884). The Harris Soda Shop burned and was replaced by the Route 66 restaurant.

Chapter 17

PEARL OTTO WESCOTT AND THE STAR THEATRE

STAR THEATRE BUILDING
44 COTTAGE STREET

The Star Theatre, a silent movie theater on Cottage Street, was seven years old when owner Joel "Joe" Emery hired his most valuable employee, Pearl Otto. Pearl was born in 1893 to William T. Otto and Isadora "Dora" Pendleton in Waltham, Massachusetts. William was an engineer from Nova Scotia who died at the age of thirty-three in 1902 of peritonitis. Pearl's mother later married Bar Harbor resident George W. Tracy on August 29, 1908, in Bar Harbor. Pearl's stepfather, who lived on Ledgelawn Avenue, was the captain of millionaire Edgar Scott's boat for several years. He was a carpenter by trade and private chauffeur.

Pearl began working in Bar Harbor around 1912 in various music-related jobs after graduating from the Philadelphia Academy of Music with the highest honors. She provided music lessons from her apartment at 37 Rodick Street and worked as the organist for the Bar Harbor Methodist Church on School Street, which was built in 1888 and later torn down in the last decades of the twentieth century. Pearl also worked as the pianist in the John Wanamaker store in Philadelphia in 1914.

Emery was not the first person to show movies in Bar Harbor. In 1900, "moving pictures showing exact reproduction" of the great Jeffries-Fizsimmons boxing match of 1899 were shown at the Music Hall.[132] In 1903, C.E. Lindall, well-known solo cornetist from Boston and leader of Lindall's military band, presented Keith's moving pictures with illustrated songs with cornet solos. A year later, Collins Famous Moving Pictures were shown at

A HISTORY LOVER'S GUIDE TO BAR HARBOR

44 Cottage Street (stop no. 17), the former Star Theatre building, which is now used for retail stores and restaurants. *Courtesy of the author.*

the Casino. In 1907, Lindall showed movies at the Music Hall with changing movies twice a week for "only five and ten cents" with "illustrated songs sung by Frank Anthony."[133] He also provided moving picture tours over the next few years as he drove through the East Coast of the United States with his movie picture apparatus, dynamo and a big string of incandescent lamps.

The Star Theatre began as a partnership among Joe Emery, Otha Jellison and John Herlihy when they leased a lot of land owned by the Rodick Realty Company and hired E.K. Whitaker to build a "modest theater" for $2,100 in 1908. The marquee added later to the front of the theater cost more than the original building construction. Essential to a silent movie nickelodeon was music to accompany the action of the film, so the theater owners bought the secondhand piano that was used at the old Rodick House from Thomas Moran. The clever businessmen bought the piano, which originally cost $1,800, for only $100. The movie projector cost $225, and the total investment of the partners was $5,000. Much of the money was said to have come from illegal liquor sales.

After buying out his partners in 1910, Emery bought a new $10,000 organ to provide live music. He installed a system of lights in the theater and "a fan back of his picture screen, which is guaranteed to change the air in the

The Star Theatre around 1919. *Courtesy of the Bar Harbor Historical Society.*

theater every five minutes."[134] He added the marquee, sloped the floor and expanded the depth to 170 feet. Seating was expanded to six hundred seats.

Emery did not have much serious competition during his years owning the theater. There was a theater in P.H. Joy's building on Main Street that started around 1908 but closed two years later. Another "tent show" was in operation for a time opposite the Star Theatre on Cottage Street, and the Casino showed movies but focused on live performances.

By the summer of 1915, movies were shown every night at the Casino, J.A. Guthrie and Sons' Airdome and the Star Theatre. The Airdome opened in 1915 on Cottage Street with a new wooden floor and a large tent across from the Star Theatre, most likely in the same spot where movies were shown earlier. Pearl Otto was the organist of the Airdome, which gave an air of class to the new theater. At the end of the season, Joe Emery hired Pearl for the Star Theatre when organist Hilda Hodgkins left Bar Harbor in 1916 to pursue an acting career.

After playing the piano that Emery purchased to replace the old Rodick House piano in 1916, Pearl had the great opportunity in July 1924 to play on his new organ, the $25,000 Robert Morgan four-manual organ, which was the largest organ in Maine. She mastered every sound effect and function of this amazing instrument. A silent movie in Bar Harbor was an auditory experience due to Pearl's masterful playing. Her playing was so popular in Bar Harbor that she was often asked to perform at private dinner parties and was organist at St. Saviour's Episcopal Church.

The great organ was considered a community asset, and Emery used the film *The Covered Wagon* to display the power of the new organ and the talent of his organist. The movie called "for everything in accompanying music that may express human emotion, in grief or joy, in the stress of danger, in the peace of home and the stress and strain, the bravery, the pathos, the hope, the fear, that comes with the trials of crossing those miles and miles of prairie."[135] Pearl's "superb combination of majestic chords of the organ with the clear, sweet notes of the violin, the flute, the cornet, every instrument which makes up a great orchestra, all were shown in perfect beauty."[136]

C. William Chilman recalled watching Pearl play in a *Down East Magazine* article in January 1969 about his childhood experiences at the Star Theatre. He called her "a genius, the high priestess of a vanished and peculiarly American skill," and said that she entered the theater five minutes before the movie began. After Pearl sat down, she "coaxed the maximum of appropriate sound from this great organ" with "one eye on the screen a mere 12 feet away and the other on her sheet music, her keys and her stops."[137] Chilman commended her "split second timing in adapting her finger work to the action and mood of the movie"; perfect selection of music as the story unfolded; ability to play "exactly the right time span and with just the right degree of emotion"; and skill of transitions from scene to scene with shifting themes, "transposing smoothly without a break, always blending music and action in one continuous form."[138] He was also amazed at how she "never failed to pick the right tune" and that her depth of knowledge of various types of music, including "jazz, the classics or Victor Herbert—even hornpipes, jigs and *The Indian Love Call* was exceptional."[139]

Pearl Otto Wescott with the Morgan organ at the Star Theatre in the 1920s. *Courtesy of the Bar Harbor Historical Society.*

In January 1926, Pearl Otto's great talent was recognized when she was invited to play at a "musicale" and tea in New York City hosted by Mrs. Frederick Vanderbilt. The guest of honor at this function was Prince Paul of Greece, and the soloist was the well-known contralto Emma Roberts, who played in the homes of summer residents of Bar Harbor often the previous season.[140] Pearl's work "always won favor" with Mrs. Vanderbilt, who heard her play in Bar Harbor, and her invitation to play at her musicale was "marked recognition of the Bar Harbor musician's ability."[141]

On March 24, 1926, Pearl Otto and Frederick Wescott were married at St. Luke's Cathedral in Portland. Besides the job at the theater, Pearl was organist and director of music at the Bar Harbor Congregational Church, and her new husband was organist and director of music at St. Saviour's Episcopal Church and a member of several male quartets. Wescott was a war veteran, stationed in France, and was a member of George Edwin Kirk American Legion Post.

Pearl Otto Wescott took her usual six-week break from Bar Harbor during the winter months. During her vacation, Edwin Cleaves played the organ at the Star Theatre. Newspaper notices reported that she traveled to Newport, Rhode Island, and Hawaii with musical events.

In January 1929, Emery signed "the only five-year franchise that Paramount has ever granted a Maine theatre."[142] The contract was signed in the New York offices of Paramount Famous Lasky Corporation after months of negotiations with Al Bevin of Portland, manager for Paramount, and other important executives of the corporation. Emery agreed to buy and exhibit every picture produced by Paramount, including Paramount News and short subjects, as well as feature films, within thirty days of their release dates. The Star Theatre was granted exclusive rights to show Paramount pictures in Bar Harbor for five years, and no other Mount Desert Island theater could show any Paramount picture until at least fourteen days after its first showing at the theater.

Emery made his largest capital investment in May 1929 by installing Western Electric Sound equipment in the Star Theatre that supported both the Vitaphone and the Movietone sound films. Even though the new system could handle sound pictures both from records and from films, Pearl's organ playing was still part of the preshow and postshow. Many people looked forward to her playing before the movie started.

In March 1930, after many successful performances of the Star Theatre organ accompanying silent movies, Emery decided to give the town a display of the full beauty of the organ with a Sunday hourlong musical performance to show the "perfection of its many remarkable attributes," including "mechanical detail, power, witness, and quality of tone," along with the talent of his organist, Wescott.[143] The Sunday program was "well balanced from the musical point of view" and "made up of almost entirely of classic music," which appealed to "all tastes, whether to the student of organ music, or to one who loves it without having studied it."[144]

Joel "Joe" Arthur Emery died on July 7, 1930, while recovering from a mastoid operation at the Eastern Maine General Hospital in Bangor. The newspaper obituary spoke about the shock to the community of his passing and how people from various "walks of life" and "ages" "expressed deep regret for the loss of someone who was a friend to everyone."[145] Emery was a redheaded, blue-eyed hometown boy who attended local public schools and worked in the plumbing trade before becoming a theater owner. People noted his community activities using his great building to help the Red Cross, the poor, the elderly, children and people in need. Emery was said to be "an interesting companion" even though he was "a reserved man of a few words."[146] Some accounts say that his memorial service was at the theater with his body on the stage as Pearl Otto Wescott played the amazing organ that he purchased for the theater six years before.

After Emery's death, his brother Oscar took over management of the theater, and 1932 was the last big year for the Star Theatre. After the opening of the art deco dream place the Criterion Theatre (35 Cottage Street), the theater hobbled along for the rest of the season. In September 1932, manager Abe Goldsmith of Orono stated, "I am sorry to close the Star and know that many theatre patrons will miss the popular playhouse, yet it is necessary at this time. We shall offer the best of shows at the Criterion and hope that Star patrons may feel at home in this splendid theatre."[147] Like the Star Theatre, the Criterion was said to be financed by bootlegging money and had a speakeasy in the basement.

The theater reopened in 1933 as Geo. C. McKay's Star Theatre. It thrived as an additional screen for movies during the summer months for the next few years. The ads for the Criterion and the Star were positioned next to each other in the *Bar Harbor Times*. The Criterion, called an "ultra-modern theatre," had the more top-line features, and the Star had the B productions and serials like *Rin Tin Tin*.

Anna Ryan remembered going to the Star Theatre in the early 1930s as a child. It cost fifteen cents and the Criterion was thirty-five cents, so the kids chose the Star. First-run features were on Sunday, and on Saturday afternoon were serials. The Star sold popcorn from a machine, but no drinks were allowed in the theater. Anna recalled that patrons entered the theater, sat down with their friends and waited for the organ music to start. Pearl Wescott played music regularly, with Shirley Johnson (Ash) filling in when she was on vacation. The kids could not wait for Pearl to walk down the aisle and sit down at the large organ because then they knew the movie was about to start and the lights would dim very slowly. If it was a double feature, you had to exit the theater from one of the side exit doors. Anna said that the theater interior was simple, and that is why the Criterion Theatre was such an upgrade for the town.

A fire that appeared to be suspicious in January 1935 caused limited damage to the building. The theater was no longer called the Geo. C. McKay's Star Theatre in 1935 or 1936 but was open for the whole year with Oscar Emery as manager. This business must not have been successful since it did not reopen in 1937.

In 1938, George McKay renovated the theater into the Star Nite Lounge, which lasted a couple of years. He added dormer windows and built ten "light and attractively decorated rooms" on the second floor with a wide corridor running between the entrance of the rooms that McKay used to show motion pictures to the screen, which was "kept in condition for this purpose" for "private motion picture shows."[148]

The largest floor space was on the lower level, which included the dance floor surrounded by chairs with paper garlands on the walls and ceiling. At the end of the floor was the organ that Pearl was hired to play at formal gatherings at the club. McKay's kitchen chef was Bithen Tripp, and 232 people attended the opening in 1938.

Little appeared in the *Bar Harbor Times* about the Star Nite Lounge after 1938. McKay later used the hotel for apartments and the lounge for private and public events. Constance Ells had her twelfth birthday party at the Star Nite Lounge in February 1939, after which refreshments and games were enjoyed.[149] In August 1939, the Townsend Club had a banquet there.

The building became the Bar Harbor Bowling Academy in 1941. This bowling alley was a big part of the town activities for the next fourteen years,

Twelfth birthday party of Constance Ells at Star Nite Lounge in February 1939 with Dorothy Kirk, Sylvia Young, Jessie Alexander, Peggy Ingalls, Martha Rodick, Marian Stanley, Eleanor Griffiths, Geraldine Baker, Marion Russell, Natalie Stout, Carolyn Alley, Evelyn Megguire and Charlotte Roberts. *Courtesy of the author.*

with various leagues playing at the alley with local bowling legends like Boogie Grindle. In 1949, Emery's $28,000 mortgage from 1929 to pay for the sound system was fully paid and discharged. The bowling alley closed in 1955, which was the same year Oscar Emery died and the Star Theatre Inc. transferred the building and another piece of property to his wife, Helen B. Emery. The "centrally located building, equipment and large corner lot"[150] was up for sale in August 1956 from the Lyman Company.

The roof of the center part of the building collapsed during a snowstorm in the late 1950s but was not repaired. A month after Helen B. Emery sold the Star property to Bernard "Bun" Cough Sr. on March 23, 1959, a letter to the editor in the *Bar Harbor Times* on April 23 complained that the building was "so ugly in its ruins" and "part of it" looked like it was "ready to fall down, with a little wind."[151] There was a proposal in a town meeting to buy the Star Theatre property for $10,000 to widen Rodick Street, which the warrant committee recommended to indefinitely postpone in September 1959.[152]

Bun Cough renovated the building and moved his Main Street store that specialized in new and damaged furniture to the Star Theatre site on Cottage Street in December 1960. In 1972, Cough sold the building to Morton Sachsman, whose son opened the Yankee Peddler a few years earlier. Other stores such as All Fired Up Art Gallery and Art Studio and Simply Natural, Alpaca, Sheepskin, Bamboo have been located at this address.

The middle section of the building where the roof collapsed was where the dance floor and seats had been located. Today, a restaurant uses this space in the building. In the back part of the building where the stage and the Emery apartment were located is where the Lompoc Café restaurant is today.

Pearl Otto Wescott later taught music to many town residents, worked as a music buyer for Andrews Music House and was organist at St. Saviour's Episcopal Church in Bar Harbor. She also performed at private recitals and dinner parties at Frederick Vanderbilt's Sonogee (1903) and at the Rockefellers' home in Seal Harbor into her eighties.

The organ was moved when the Star Theatre closed to the private residence of William Deacon, owner of Andrews Music House, before being donated to the Hauck Memorial Auditorium at the University of Maine in 1969. Debbie Dyer from the Bar Harbor Historical Society said that she was contacted by someone in California who now has the organ and was restoring it. The white-and-gold Star Theatre sign is owned by Raymond Strout of Bar Harbor. Roy Blake, the projectionist at the Star Theatre, later worked as the projector operator and assistant manager at the Criterion Theatre for many years.

Although Joel Emery was not there for the opening of the Criterion Theatre in 1932, the movie audience that he developed in Bar Harbor for nearly twenty-five years ensured the success of the new theater. He taught moviegoers about the new medium of film and showed them the evolution of motion pictures from eleven-minute shorts to full-length sound movies. He introduced them to unknown French actors who were later replaced by the Hollywood star system and top-rate directors and producers. Emery gave them the best technology over the years, which gave them the urge to want more as they sat in the dark theater. He helped them see motion pictures develop to an art form, and his love for the film endures on Cottage Street with the Criterion Theatre and the Star Theatre building at the corner of Rodick and Cottage Streets.

Bonus Historical Site: Former Bar Harbor Police Station/Coston & McIssac CPAs (38 Rodick Street, 1935).

Chapter 18

RAGS TO RICHES: HOW PEANUT ROW BECAME THE HARBORSIDE HOTEL

WHALE WATCH BUILDING (CLARK COAL COMPANY BUILDING) 55 WEST STREET

Peanut Row was built in the mid-1880s on the land owned by Fountain and Serenus Rodick. The Rodicks also owned the land of the "Back Yard" across the street. The area included land between Rodick Street and Billings Avenue on the Frenchman Bay side of West Street. The Milliken Coal Company and later the Clark Coal Company was its neighbor to the right going toward the municipal pier. The Whale Watch Building was a Clark Coal Company office building from the early twentieth century. The Edgar L. Roberts Coal and Wood Company was its neighbor on the left to the rear. This area was later owned by Frank Spratt and the Clark Coal Company. For much of its early existence, Peanut Row was in the shadow of the West End Hotel, which towered over it across the street on West Street in the area framed by the two entrances to Billings Avenue. Peanut Row was possibly developed to provide housing for the workers of the large hotels and other summer businesses.

An 1885 J.E. Hilgard map of Bar Harbor shows the neighborhood with at least nine houses and with its own road to Frenchman Bay from West Street. The *Bar Harbor Mount Desert Herald* of April 29, 1887, reported, "Mr. Amos Hodgkins is building a three-tenement block at the extreme end of Peanut Row…[and] on the same row, Mr. Artell A. Moseley, of Trenton, is building a small house 20 by 20 feet, with two rooms on each of two floors and a basement consisting of the kitchen and pantry" with shingle exterior. The people who owned property on Peanut Row in 1886–87, according to

55 West Street (stop no. 18), Whale Watch Building (former Clark Coal Company building), Harborside Hotel. *Courtesy of the author.*

Peanut Row and Milliken Coal, Wood and Charcoal Company (later Clark Coal Company), 1880s. *Courtesy of Southwest Harbor Library.*

the 1887 Colby Map, included the following names: Pendleton, Harrington, Grant, Clarke, Tyrrel and McDown.

The fact that the term "Peanut Row" is used in the article indicates that this name was familiar to the locals concerning the neighborhood prior to 1887. The neighborhood was considered the closest thing in Bar Harbor to an urban slum. Prayer meetings were held every Wednesday in 1893 by the Woman's Christian Temperance Union. The need for these meetings revealed that alcohol and violence against women were issues in the neighborhood.

An assault occurred there in 1894 when Joseph Courts was hit three times in the head for cheating with Samuel Stover's wife, who was a maid. Stover threatened to "smash Courts head" before leaving on a fishing trip. When he returned, he found "his unfaithful wife with her lover in his house."[153] With a heavy stick, he hit Courts in the head three times, opening the scalp to the bone. He was arrested, but the judge dismissed the charges since Courts did not appear in court.

An 1895 article described Peanut Row on the road called Bayview Road as

> *a boulevard, about one hundred feet long, forty feet wide at one end and ten at the other. On the right side are eight structures, on the left seven and at the farther end, one, which abruptly shuts off further progress. Peanut Row looking north from West Street, looks quaint, and especially is this true on a Monday morning when the little front yards are filled with waving shirts and an aggregation of unmentionables. A few scraggly flowers and shrubs grow on the left side; the right is barren of vegetation, the only appearance of life being the baby with its dirty face and hands and a dog or two. The view from any back door looks out upon a miscellaneous collection of barrels, tin cans and ashes. The end house is built over a dirty wharf which at low water commands an excellent view of the mud flats, but beyond are the shores and islands of Frenchman's Bay.*[154]

One newspaper article joked that "society on Peanut Row is not unlike that of the wealthy of Bar Harbor"[155] with their regular series of entertainments every day of the week. Monday is "a glow with the sport of washing clothes. Tuesday afternoon they have an accordion symphony. On Wednesday there is a wake superintended by Mr. Patrick Conley."[156]

The Republican presidential victory of William McKinley in November 1896 was celebrated on Peanut Row by "a bonfire and a string of Chinese lanterns across its entrance."[157] In 1897, the BHVIA reported that "an alley known as Peanut row, inhabited by about 40 persons, proved to be in such a viciously unsanitary state that your committee insisted upon its renovation and upon the laying of sewer pipe throughout its length," which was "accomplished and all the houses have been connected."[158] A Collector's Notice and Advertisement of the Sale of Lands of Non-Residential Owners for unpaid 1897 property taxes in the *Bar Harbor Record* in November 1898 included the Mosley house on Peanut Row.[159]

A doctor described the birth of a baby on Peanut Row in the late 1800s. He was called at midnight to a Peanut Row "hovel" and found a woman suffering from second-stage labor. He asked for a nurse, and the patient said that she did not have one. Her "poor specimen of a husband" was called but "could not get a nurse because he had never paid a bill in his life."[160] The baby was born with a "deformed skull and died 4 months later."[161]

A fire occurred in 1910 when a few buildings burned and a "number of women gathered upon the roof of a small building near to view the flames."[162] The "old and unsafe" building collapsed; twenty women were thrown to the ground, and one woman was seriously injured and taken to the hospital.[163] The term "women" emphasized in the newspaper item seems to hint that they may have been prostitutes. The existence of such establishments had been rumored in the area.

In 1911, the major fire at the Frank Spratt Lumber Yard property next to Peanut Row destroyed ten to twelve of the buildings in the community. This is the last time the neighborhood is mentioned in the newspaper and may signal when the area was transformed from a residential to an industrial area with warehouses, small buildings and the town dump. Postcards of the section during the 1920s show a very industrial landscape.

Spratt was paid during the late 1910s for using his land and some of the Peanut Row land as a dump for the town trash. This dumping contract, which also included burning trash and dumping ash and other garbage in Frenchman Bay near Bald Porcupine Island, was continued by Robert McKay, the Clark Coal Company and others during the late 1910s and 1920s. The granite retaining wall on Frenchman Bay was built to keep the trash from ending up in the water. A metal fence surrounded the perimeter of the site. The dump was closed in the late 1920s when the Bar Harbor Club was established; the town wanted to make the area safe for swimming.

The Back Yard was the area bordered by West Street to the north, Main on the east, Cottage on the south and Rodick on the west. It was considered part of Peanut Row at the turn of the century but developed a better reputation in the early twentieth century as more working-class people lived in the area. When Peanut Row disappeared, the Back Yard became the low-income housing in the wharf area. Although Dr. John B. Ells always said he grew up in Peanut Row, his father's business and possibly his residence were at the southeast corner of Rodick and West Streets at the beginning of the Back Yard. Today, the Back Yard is the site of the new West Street Hotel and other businesses.

The Golden Anchor Motel was built on the Peanut Row/industrial site and other adjacent lots as part of the rebuilding of the resort town after the Fire of 1947. The eighty-eight-unit motel was built in 1968 with a swimming pool on the property. There was also the Golden Anchor Pier Restaurant and the Golden Anchor Friendship Sloop at the flying bridge pier. Lorenzo Creamer Jr., Leslie Brewer and other local businessmen were involved in this venture to improve the area. Over the years, the motel expanded, whale-watching and a gift shop were added and Creamer eventually became the sole owner of the business.[164]

In the early 2000s, the Golden Anchor was replaced by the Harborside Hotel, Spa and Marina. Ocean Properties built a six-thousand-square-foot addition to the Golden Anchor costing $500,000, converted the former restaurant into four hotel guest suites and erected seven "retail shacks" on the pier along the concourse that connects the pier to West Street. The hotel has 187 guest rooms and suites, all of which have marble bathrooms, semi-private balconies and down pillows and comforters.

Obviously, the neighborhood has improved over the last 140 years.

Chapter 19

THE WEST END HOTEL AND THE BAR HARBOR CLUB

BAR HARBOR CLUB
111 WEST STREET

The West End Hotel that towered over the surrounding buildings on West Street was one of the first large buildings that visitors saw when visiting Bar Harbor in the late 1800s. Although the frontage of the hotel was on West Street (sometimes called West End Avenue) with grounds beginning near today's West Street Café location, the large hotel sprawled deep into the land between West and Cottage Streets. The area between the first and second entrances to Billings Avenue on West Street today follows half of the footprint of the hotel. The rest went farther into the land on the left of Billings Avenue toward Cottage Street.

The first Billings Avenue entrance is also the road that once went all the way through to Cottage Street in the 1890s. Originally, the road only looped near the hotel. In the late 1890s, the road was expanded toward Cottage Street, which made the hotel one of the most accessible hotels during this era. The road took a bend to the left as it was extended toward Cottage Street following the part of Federal Street to the right of the post office near the property line. This was before the Federal Road box was created when the Bar Harbor Post Office (55 Cottage Street) was built in 1909.

Although West Street was often known for the low-income residential housing and businesses in this area near the wharf in the late 1800s, upper West Street had a very different reputation due to the West End Hotel and the cottages built toward Eden Street as the road expanded in length. The opening of the swimming club and later the Bar Harbor Club after the

111 West Street (stop no. 19), former location of the Bar Harbor Swimming Club, which is today part of the Harborside Hotel, Spa and Marina. *Courtesy of the author.*

West End Hotel's demise enhanced the area's reputation even more with the wealthy set.

The West End Hotel was built on a plot of land on the south side of West Street in 1878–79 and opened in 1880. Records show that the land of the "Haywood House Lot" was sold to Oren M. Shaw and his son Fred A. Shaw (O.M. Shaw & Son),[165] who also owned the Falmouth Hotel in Portland, by James P. Armbrust, a famous photographer and Vinalhaven granite quarry owner. The hotel was eventually expanded to include rooms for four hundred people with a fine orchestra for the season. The exterior included "pretty lawns studded with fountains and rockeries" and entrances from West and Cottage Streets.[166]

In the 1880s and 1890s, the hotel was refurbished to include "modern improvements" such as "perfect drainage, electric lights, electric bells, gas, elevator, baths, steam heat, steam laundry, fire alarm, fire escapes, etc."[167] In 1889, the hotel underwent "extensive interior decoration," making it the "finest specimen of Moresque decoration of any hotel in America," according to hotel advertisements. Famous architect Bruce Price, who designed the Chateau Frontenac in Quebec City and the Turrets in Bar Harbor (now College of the Atlantic), designed the annex for the West End Hotel.

Rooms included suites with or without baths and private parlors. Rates for board were three to four dollars per day, fifteen to twenty-five dollars per week, according to location of room and season. In 1881, the hotel staff included a clerk, C.W. Wormell, and a cashier, F.W. Adams.

In the spring of 1888, O.M. Shaw, "proprietor of the West End Hotel," visited his "intimate friend" James Blaine, famous Maine politician and presidential candidate in 1884, in Florence, Italy. Blaine went to Florence to get away from the kingmakers urging him to run for president. After his return in April, Shaw created controversy when he told the *Bangor Dispatch* that Blaine had health issues with diabetes and stomach ailments and would not run for president.[168] The Maine Republican political establishment fought to refute the claim, and Shaw had to retract this statement. It was not reported if the issue hurt the friendship between Shaw and Blaine or whether Blaine leaked the health information to avoid running for president. The Republican convention in June 1888 in Chicago selected Benjamin Harrison as the Republican candidate while Blaine remained in Europe. Harrison went on to defeat President Cleveland in the November election and appointed Blaine as his secretary of state.

The "changing guest preferences and travel patterns" in the 1890s hurt the business of the West End Hotel and other large Bar Harbor hotels.[169] To make matters worse, a land dispute in the 1890s that involved the ownership of the three lots that made up the property of the hotel brought an end to the venerable hotel. The hotel was sold to C.B. Dalton of Dalton & Co. of Portland and was razed in January 1900.

It was estimated that 500,000 feet of lumber and six hundred windows and doors were "carted to the wharf and shipped by vessel to Portland" to be used for construction of "another hotel at Cape Elizabeth" and "the erection of cottages there."[170] The quality of the wood from buildings of this era was usually outstanding and was cut from trees that started to grow in the 1700s or from old-growth forests.[171] A "large amount" of "kindling wood" was also available for local people to "have a chance to get a liberal supply at a reasonable price."[172]

The Rodick House demolition in 1907 was said to have recycled fifty thousand lathes (boards).[173] They also sold two hundred of the "very best curled hair mattresses, three hundred chamber sets, six hundred chairs, a lot of Rogers Brothers Silver ware, Glass ware, crockery, carpets, bedding, tables, most everything needed in a house for housekeeping."[174] A similar inventory of items must have been sold when the West End Hotel was closed.

Forty-two-year-old Charles C. Linscott fell off the roof during the demolition and was seriously injured. He recovered from his injuries and later that year became a hotelkeeper on School Street in Bar Harbor.[175] O.M. Shaw died in Winthrop, Maine, on January 30, 1900, after his old hotel was razed. Shaw's son Fred A. Shaw went on to own other hotels in the states of Maine and New York.

C.B. Dalton bought the Cliff Cottage property in Cape Elizabeth near Portland in 1899 from Alpheus Hyatt, the famous U.S. zoologist and paleontologist, and renamed it Cliff House. Besides Cliff House, he owned the surrounding land called Ottawa Park, which most likely received its name due to the hotel's popularity with Canadian tourists.[176] Portland civil engineer Harry Taylor Harmon created a subdivision plan for fifty-six cottage lots surrounding the hotel.[177]

Dalton used the lumber and other materials from the West End Hotel for a major renovation of venerable 1873 Cliff House, which expanded to one hundred rooms; the construction of Glenn Cottage, which was an annex to the hotel; and the construction of some of the Ottawa Park cottages between 1900 and 1914 when he served as treasurer of the Ottawa Park Company. In 1906, Dalton sold the Cliff House property to E. Benson Stanley, who also owned the Stanley House in Southwest Harbor (Manset). Stanley renovated Cliff House with a lower floor reconstructing the music room and introduced an English tearoom.[178]

The Ottawa Park Company continued to build cottages and was still a functioning entity in 1911 when it conveyed land on Seaview Avenue to the town as public land by the beach. Stanley expanded the hotel to make it a year-round hotel by installing modern heating systems and adding an additional seventy-five rooms. The hotel was consumed by fire in 1914, and later, the land became the site of several houses.[179]

In 1910, the West End Hotel lot on West Street was sold as small lots for homes and businesses. Today, residences and some stores are located on the site of the former hotel. The reuse of timber and building materials of hotels, houses and barns during the Victorian era was extensive. Many of the homes built in Bar Harbor and other Maine towns during this era included the wood from earlier buildings. Like the recycling of ancient Roman marbles and statues during the Renaissance era in Italy, this process gave new life to these materials and reminds us that the 400-room West End Hotel (razed 1900), the 700-room Rodick House (razed 1906), the 350-room Grand Central (razed 1899) and other Bar Harbor hotels from this era that did not succumb to fire are quite possibly part

West End Hotel, 1880s. *Courtesy of the Bar Harbor Historical Society.*

of homes and other buildings existing today in the town and other towns in Maine.

The Bar Harbor Club was made up of three major properties: Bar Harbor Swimming Club, the estate of Tobias L. Roberts and the Frank Spratt plot. The different functions of these properties, including affluent recreation, residential land and industrial/sanitation, reflected the complicated nature of West Street in the late nineteenth and early twentieth centuries.

The Bar Harbor Swimming Club was founded in 1903 on the land of Mrs. Daniel Hinckley called the "Pemetic Lodge." The club was one of the pillars of Bar Harbor summer society during the first three decades of the twentieth century. By the late 1920s, club president Phillip Livingston and the facilities were considered "old fashioned" by Bar Harbor summer society leaders Edward "Ned" T. Stotesbury, Potter Palmer and A. Atwater Kent.[180]

After Tobias L. Roberts passed away in 1908, his family sold several of his principal property holdings, including the Rockaway House. This lot on West Street was another shoreline lot that the Roberts family owned for several years. The function of the lot is not evident in maps of the era, which show a house near the water and a barn. The lot was half the size of the swimming club lot.

Frank Spratt had a lumberyard and later a dump on part of his property that was later used for the club. After Spratt's death in 1920 and establishment of a new dumping site by the town, this lot became available. Many in the town were happy to see this blighted area of West Street cleaned up.

At the time of the 1929 stock market crash, a fund was established to build the Bar Harbor Club. A. Atwater Kent, inventor and radio manufacturer, pledged $25,000, and the founding members were able to raise $262,550 in the first year of the Great Depression. Construction began in October 1929 with a design by architect Bradley Delehanty of New York. It was completed by July 1, 1930, and opened with "the grandest ball the island had ever seen" on July 4, 1930.[181]

The Bar Harbor Club consisted of the clubhouse on West Street, a fresh-water pool, nine tennis courts and a saltwater pool. The club offered "meals, rooms to relax while playing cards or smoking cigars, fresh and saltwater swimming pools, tennis courts and a grand ballroom for dances."[182] The club had a peak membership in 1930 of 150 members with annual dues of $18,000. Membership was controlled, and very few locals were invited to join. Presidents of the Bar Harbor Club during the 1930s and 1940s included Edward T. Stotesbury, Potter Palmer and Major George McMurtry. During this era, all of resort society gathered before

Bar Harbor Swim Club, early 1900s. *Courtesy of the Bar Harbor Historical Society.*

lunch on Sundays during the season at the Bar Harbor Club.[183] In 1938, Bar Harbor had its liveliest Independence Day weekend in years, which included the formal opening of the Bar Harbor Club with the first of its weekly Sunday evening buffet suppers and numerous dinners and cocktail parties at the various residences.

The Great Depression, World War II and the Fire of 1947 forever changed the nature of Bar Harbor society. By 1981, the membership of the organization had expanded to include town residents and had 130 members.[184] This expansion could not save the club. Membership decreased, and the building became vacant and deteriorated for many years. Local people felt the building was destined to be razed and replaced by a modern structure.

In 2009, the historic private club "dating back to the Rockefellers, Pulitzers and Vanderbilts in the early 1900s" was refurnished by Ocean Properties. The historic clubhouse with "7,000 square feet of function space" was restored as "a state-of-the-art full-service Spa."[185] A two-story pool house and the outdoor pool were also built and restored as part of the project.

In July 2010, President Obama visited the restored Bar Harbor Club during his visit to Bar Harbor. The first family "played some tennis and hung out at the pool."[186] The presidential visit was acknowledgement of the successful restoration of the building, which is listed in the National Register of Historic Places. All these changes to this section of Bar Harbor have reestablished the reputation of the town for the good things in life—if you can afford them. The new development and restoration of West Street have also renewed its role as a beacon for arriving visitors to Bar Harbor, as it was over 140 years ago.

Other West Street Sites: Thankful Cottage (1 Billings Avenue, 1850); Manor House Inn (106 West Street, 1887), Foster Cottage (108 West Street, 1878); Petunia Cottage (110 West Street, 1887); Guelph/Rosebriar (111 West Street, 1875); The Kedge (112 West Street, 1870); Sunset (115 West Street, 1911); Chantier (116 West Street, 1887); Maisonette (118 West Street, 1886); The Tides (119 West Street, 1887); Westfield (120 West Street, 1901); Saltair (121 West Street, 1887); Greenlawn (123 West Street, 1884); The Breezes (125 West Street, 1900); and Charles Marinke residence (130 West Street, 1912).

Chapter 20

DR. JOHN B. ELLS AND THE OBE

LA ROCHELLE/BAR HARBOR HISTORICAL SOCIETY 127 WEST STREET

During the Second World War, Bar Harbor became a hub for North Atlantic naval activity for the Allies. American, Canadian and British ships regularly docked in Bar Harbor. For many of the men on these ships, a trip to Bar Harbor made the difficult task of war a little bearable and recharged their batteries. As chairman of the Warships Committee, Dr. John B. Ells met with the captains of each ship and welcomed them to the town. He organized dances and other services for the sailors. In time of war, this became a symbol of national pride and economic opportunity to the local community. Dr. Ells became the symbol of Bar Harbor's welcome mat to the world, and he was called "the poor man's Grover Whalen," the official greeter for the City of New York for many years.[187]

Dr. Ells later recalled:

> *Some people were afraid that our American boys would get into squabbles with the British so I thought if we staged some fights it would be a good way to get any such tendencies out of their systems. Both navies had the time of their lives, and our boys hired the back side of Bar Island and gave a big party for the English gobs with steamed clams, hot-dogs, hamburgers and so much beer that it was passed around in watering sprinklers.*[188]

Some of his British visitors remarked that Ells looked like their prime minister, Winston Churchill. Dr. Ells responded by saying, "Lots of people say I look like Churchill, dear. If you want to know what I think, I think Churchill is the homeliest old curmudgeon I ever saw."[189]

127 West Street (stop no. 20), the Bar Harbor Historical Society at La Rochelle. *Courtesy of the Bar Harbor Historical Society.*

During World War II, the Casino became the meeting hall, dance hall and public area for the town. At one of Dr. Ells's dances for the British sailors, a drunken sailor was approached by him and the shore police to make sure he was removed from the hall for intoxication. The drunken sailor grabbed both sides of Dr. Ells's straw hat and pulled it down over his face like a vaudeville act, to the amusement of the crowd. Ells did not hold it against the man and retold the story many times since it involved the navy and a good joke about himself, which he loved.

Although he brought many ships to Bar Harbor, Dr. Ells felt his greatest achievement was to make a trip to Washington in 1946 to consult with U.S. senators and representatives, which resulted in the coming to Bar Harbor that summer of the USS *Missouri*. All the world saw the pictures and read the headlines about the Japanese surrender on the deck of the *Missouri* a year earlier. To have such a well-known vessel come to Bar Harbor excited the town, created news and brought tourists with money to the town to visit the ship.

In 1955, Queen Elizabeth II awarded Dr. Ells his greatest honor, the Member of the Most Excellent Order of the British Empire in "recognition of services in the cause of Anglo-American friendship and understanding."

Above: Dr. John B. Ells being awarded the Order of the British Empire by Queen Elizabeth II at a ceremony on April 12, 1955, in Washington, D.C., with his son John Ells Jr., Percy Ells, Sir Roger Makins (British ambassador), Dr. John B. Ells and Florence Somes Ells. *Courtesy of the author.*

Left: Poster for a dance on July 7, 1943, for servicemen at the Casino sponsored by Dr. John B. Ells during World War II that had five hundred attendees. *Courtesy of the author.*

Dr. Ells was made "a member of the Order of the British Empire by QEII in recognition of his hospitality to British sailors who have been coming into Bar Harbor aboard ships for many years."[190] He traveled to Washington, D.C., and was given the award by Sir Roger Makins, the British ambassador, on April 12, 1955.

As a boy, Dr. Ells saw his first naval ships visit Bar Harbor during the annual Squadron Week each August. He once said, "I'm just kind of a nut about warships. It's my hobby. Has been ever since I visited the Battleship *Maine* when I was 6 years old in 1897. I've tried to build real friendship between the British tars and our townsfolk, usually with great success. I suppose that's the reason for the award."[191]

Ells also made the following remarks about his family's feelings about his Warship Committee activities: "She [his second wife, Florence Somes Ells] thinks and I guess my son and daughter do, too that I might have been a more prosperous man if I hadn't given so much time to the kind of behind the scenes public service."[192]

Small towns have a way of bringing you back to earth when your fortunes soar. When Dr. Ells returned to Bar Harbor from Washington, people in the streets who heard the news congratulated him on his award and gave him praise. Feeling quite high on himself, he decided to go down to the police station to hang out with his buddies. They were ready for him. When he entered the station, they began to talk about him as if he was not in the room: "Did you hear Doc Ells went to Washington to receive the OBE. The OBE? What's that? Oh you know, Old Bull**** Ells. Now I see." Dr. Ells burst out laughing, realizing that these close friends were suddenly telling him to come down to earth. To them, nothing had changed. So, after this grand chapter in his life, he returned to his normal routine with those who knew him and loved him. Ells was always close to the Bar Harbor Police Department and Police Chief Lyman Kane, who assisted him with the activities for visiting sailors and visitors.

In 1960, Dr. Ells resigned from his job as leader of the Bar Harbor GOP after thirty-five years at the helm. In 1961, he ran in a special election for state senator against Frank Dunbar of Belfast to fill out the term of a man who died in office. Dr. Ells won, capturing 80 percent of the vote on Mount Desert Island. He served as state senator until the fall of 1962. Dr. Ells passed away nine years later in December 1971.

The only other person connected with Bar Harbor to be knighted by a monarch was summer resident Morris K. Jesup, who was knighted by Czar Nicholas for his gifts to the Academy of Science at St. Petersburg, Russia.

Dr. John B. Ells signing up to support Nelson Rockefeller for president in 1968. *Courtesy of the author.*

He was honored for a series of items provided from the Jesup exploration collections. Jesup was involved with the Perry expeditions that led to the discovery of the North Pole in 1909.[193]

Dr. Ells's Order of the British Empire is on display at the Bar Harbor Historical Society at La Rochelle. The Bar Harbor Historical Society describes La Rochelle as

> *a Georgian Revival mansion built in 1902–1903 that is the only brick estate built on the ocean side of West Street in Bar Harbor. The architect was Andrews, Jaques and Rantoul of Boston and the estate was built for George Sullivan Bowdoin, great grandson of Alexander Hamilton and partner and Treasurer of J.P. Morgan. His great grandfather founded Bowdoin College in Brunswick, Maine in 1794. The property was later bought by Bun Cough who sold the property in 1944 to Tristram Colket of Philadelphia and his wife Ethel Dorrance Colket, daughter of John Thompson Dorrance, a chemist who invented condensed soup and eventually became president of the Campbell Soup Company. The Maine Seacoast Mission purchased the estate in 1972 and it served as their headquarters for the next forty-seven years. The Bar Harbor Historical Society purchased the estate in 2019. Beatrix Farrand designed and planted the original gardens at La Rochelle which can still be viewed to this day.*[194]

Chapter 21
THE CORNER OF EDEN AND WEST STREETS

DEGREGOIRE GREEN AND PLAQUE
WEST AND EDEN STREETS CORNER

The brook running out to sea at the corner of West and Eden Streets is called Eddie Brook (aka Eddy's Brook) and is known by the locals as "the guzzle." This location in Bar Harbor appears quite inactive today, with a park and some residences hidden away several feet from the road near the bridge leading into Bar Harbor from Eden Street down West Street. One hundred years earlier, this was a key commercial location in the town.

Old maps show this area being quite wild with trees, farms and little development until the 1880s. No record survives noting the builder of the general store on the side of Eddy's Brook, but by 1886, Arthur W. Ells was the proprietor. This store only lasted a few years and is usually not mentioned in the history of businesses in Bar Harbor during this era. The store was on a plot of land called the Ells Block and described as a "General Variety Store" with "fine groceries, fancy goods and small wares; tobacco and cigars; and a full line of canned goods delivered free of charge."[195] Ells, a carpenter from Nova Scotia, came to Bar Harbor in the 1870s and married a local girl. After being involved in cottage building, Ells opened a store across the street on Eden Street during the early 1880s with the help of his two brothers, Frederick and Edward. He moved to the new location in 1886.

An April 1, 1887 article in the *Bar Harbor Record* stated:

> *Mr. A.W. Ells is to build an extension to his block at Eddy's brook, which will be occupied by Dr. J.H. Wilson as a photograph gallery. The building will be forty feet long, twenty-five feet, ten feet wide at the rear*

Plaque commemorating the DeGregoire Hotel and the Great Fire of 47 at the intersection of West and Eden Streets (stop no. 21) in DeGregoire Green. *Courtesy of Richard Cough.*

end to conform to the shape of the lot. It will be one story high with a "California," or battlement, front. The new building will also include a private office where Dr. Wilson will attend to his medical clients. Mr. J.C. Pettengill is the architect and builder.[196]

When Eden decided to expand West Street to Eden Street, the traditional summer area for the Indian encampment was replaced with new cottages and docks. In 1887, an Indian encampment moved to the area behind the Ells store on Frenchman Bay. A notice in the newspaper stated that the Indians were selling "novelties, baskets, fancy grass work, seal skin goods, gulls breasts and feather work of all descriptions for sale at reasonable prices." It also noted that the "encampment is perfectly tidy and has good drainage."[197]

After his two brothers went west, Ells borrowed large sums of money in the late 1880s using the store and property on Holland Avenue as collateral, which eventually resulted in foreclosure of both properties. The expansion of West Street in 1889 to Eden Street came too late to help Ells with his doomed business venture. He moved his store near Peanut Row in the early 1890s.

In October 1889, an article in the *Bar Harbor Record* provided a bleak view of the area, calling it an "unsavory locality."[198] The article stated that the "vile atmosphere of the place is unwholesome and it would be admirable breeding place for any sort of contagious disease."[199] The shanty town behind the Ells Store had small dwellings resembling Squaw Hallow that were "scattered promiscuously over the lot and intervening space resembl[ing] a dumping ground for garbage."[200] It added that there was "no drainage in the neighborhood and as a matter of course the bed of the brook and the creek are used as a common sewer."[201]

A few years later, the Ells Block buildings were leveled and replaced by the new building by famous Bar Harbor architect and builder DeGrasse Fox as a form of village improvement. Fox was known for his work on St. Sylvia's Catholic Church (1881), Malvern Hotel (1882), Tallyrand (1888), Tanglewold (1888) and other local projects. In 1892, Fox acquired the land and planned for a structure to be known as the Eden Swimming Pool Club. This "picturesque brick and half-timbered English styled building" was to have two swimming pools for members along with "eight rentable stores to produce income for the venture."[202] The building was built from 1892 to 1893. By 1895, Fox was bankrupt, and the land and an unfinished building were sold at public auction.

George L. Wescott, local contractor and the mason for La Rochelle (Bar Harbor Historical Society), bought the property at the auction. He then sold it to W.R. Lee in 1906. Lee decided to change the function of the original building and converted it to a hotel. Lee's plan, which was designed by Andrews, Jaques and Rantoul, included renovating the former clubhouse into a European-style apartment hotel for affluent visitors who wanted to spend the summer season in Bar Harbor. The DeGregoire Hotel opened in 1907 and was named for Madame Marie Therese de Gregoire, who once owned half of Mount Desert Island. The hotel had "a superb view of the bay" with tasteful grounds, including a "formal garden, a stone bridge, the little winding stream, clusters of trees and shrubbery," which made "a charming spot of a once ugly one."[203] The 1910 four-story addition on West Street made the hotel one of the key destinations in the Bar Harbor resort.

The hotel continued to be a popular location in the resort town into the 1930s and 1940s with twenty suites/apartments each consisting of a parlor, a bath, a bedroom with its own fireplace or electric heater, a full-length mirror and a telephone. The hotel had a "spacious dining hall" that was able to seat eighty people with "white enamel, golden tint" walls and "maroon carpet."[204] The kitchen was considered "a marvel of modern ingenuity."[205]

DeGregoire Hotel, early 1900s. The hotel burned in the 1947 fire. *Courtesy of the Bar Harbor Historical Society.*

Even though the hotel was a luxury hotel advertised as the "home of comfort and refinement," the BHVIA in 1929 noted "unsightly conditions at the rear of the DeGregoire Hotel," which most likely was the sewage runoff into Frenchman Bay.[206] By the late '40s, the hotel known as the Days DeGregoire Hotel had lost its luster, offering rooms for ten and eighteen dollars a night. Several other Bar Harbor cottages in the area were razed for tax reasons during the Great Depression and after World War II.

In 1942, during a county mobilization test, an air raid warden incorrectly reported that the DeGregoire Hotel was "blown up," which was a bad omen considering its ultimate fate five years later.[207] When the Fire of 1947 reached Hulls Cove, Fire Chief Sleeper realized that it was impossible to keep the fire from Bar Harbor, and his men made a firemen's stand by wetting the area near the DeGregoire Hotel. When the fire arrived, it engulfed the hotel, and then the wind shifted north and the firemen's stand was successful in turning the fire away from West and Cottage Streets. This final destruction by fire put an end to the commercial history of the location. Ten years after the fire, Frenchman's Bay Realty Company, Inc. and Bernard Cough tried to get approval to build another hotel on the site but were denied through pressure from West Street cottage owners and other private residences surrounding the former hotel site. Houses were ultimately built near the back of the lot near the old gardens of the hotel and Indian encampment. Foundation ruins of the hotel still exist on the lot. DeGregoire Green was established on the site in 2019 with a Fire of 1947 monument dedicated "to all the men and women who worked on the fire lines and behind the scenes."

Other Eden Street and Harbor Lane Sites: Blanchfield House (37 Eden Street, 1865); Caruso (41 Eden Street, 1890); Bagatelle (75 Eden Street, 1883); Villa Mary (77 Eden Street, 1879–80); Fenwold (6 Harbor Lane, 1891); Reverie Cove (7 Harbor Lane, 1893); Greencourt (8 Harbor Lane, 1883–84); and Anchorhold (9 Harbor Lane, 1885).

Chapter 22

THE COUGHS AND THE ATLANTIC OAKES

SONNY COUGH PLAQUE BY THE ATLANTIC EYRIE LODGE
6 NORMAN ROAD

The building of the Atlantic Oakes by the Sea in the Gateway district was a fulfillment of a dream for Sonny Cough and his family. The Gateway district on either side of Route 3 (Eden Street) entering Bar Harbor from the Bar Harbor Ferry Terminal to West Street was historically the location of some of the most beautiful cottages on Frenchman Bay. Although the Cough family owned and built motels in the town, they wanted to create a special property that was on Frenchman Bay. Their goal was to integrate an existing historical cottage into a comfortable modern motel with balconies to enjoy the coastal sunrise and sunset, beautiful grounds to enjoy, amenities such as hot tubs and an indoor pool, dining options for the area that was removed from the downtown dining and proximity and transportation to the Acadia National Park.

American businessman and politician Ross Perot used to paraphrase a quote by the Roman philosopher Seneca stating that luck is when opportunity and preparation meet. The Cough family had a multigenerational preparation for the opportunities that arose in the late twentieth century for the family.

Daniel Cough, Maine's first Chinese immigrant, settled in Bernard; married a local girl, Elvira Higgins; bought land; and raised a family. He established a general store, and two of his sons, Adoniram Bird Cough (aka A. Bird Cough) and Ezra Raphael Cough (aka E.R. Cough), learned the trade before moving the business to Bar Harbor. A. Bird was great at marketing but did not have the business longevity of his younger brother Ezra, who also provided heirs to the Cough family. Ezra's wife, Gertrude Lynch, brought the Catholic faith to the family.

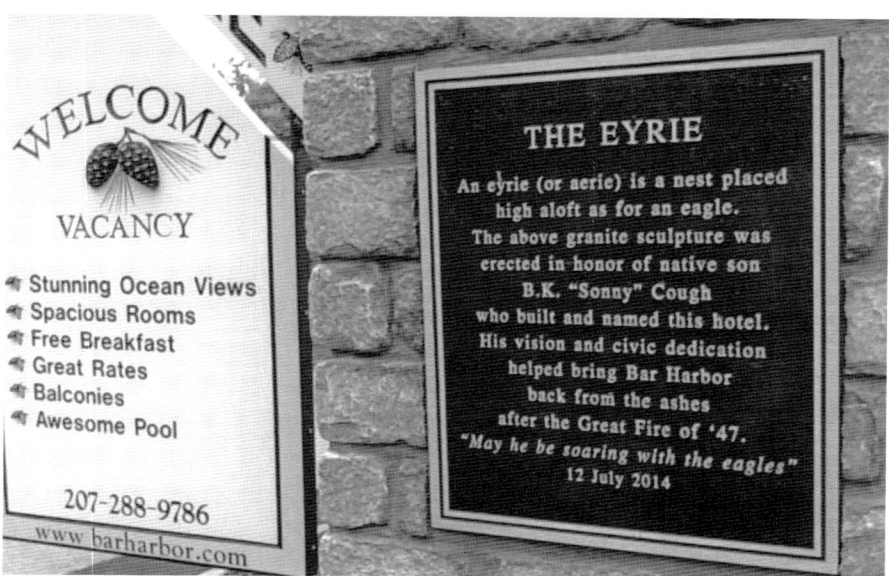

6 Norman Drive (stop no. 22), Sonny Cough plaque in front of the Atlantic Eyrie Lodge. *Courtesy of Richard Cough.*

A. Bird Cough Store at 61 Cottage Street, circa 1900. *Courtesy of Southwest Harbor Library.*

One of Ezra's sons, Bernard "Bun" Cough, was one of the most interesting businessmen in Bar Harbor history. The college graduate and former high school gym teacher laid the foundation for the Cough family success story through his constant "scheming," as his daughter Barbara called it, and his land purchases. After graduating from Farmington Normal School (now part of University of Maine), Bun married Helen Norton in Putnam, New York. Bernard Jr. "Sonny" was born on July 12, 1927, in Danbury, Connecticut. Their second son, Richard, died at seventeen months in 1929 at the Skowhegan Hospital after surgical treatment for appendicitis, followed by influenza. Barbara was born in Norridgewock in 1930, and Mary Janis and James "Jimmy" were born in Farmington in 1931 and 1933, respectively.

After saving cash during the war years, Bun saw the lemons left by the Fire of 1947 and wanted to make lemonade. He bought up much of the available land in the Gateway district with a plan to build one or more hotels. Bun owned the Stotesbury property (Wingwood, 1925) where the Bar Harbor Ferry Terminal was built. Before being razed in 1953, the Wingwood House had eighty rooms (thirty for servants), twenty-eight bathrooms, fifty-two telephones and twenty-six hand-carved marble fireplaces.[208] Bun opened the Turrets mansion as a hotel without permission from the town in 1957 and tried to break the zoning in court, which failed. Bun also tried to build a hotel on the DeGregoire Hotel site and failed. He developed other retail businesses in town with his sons, including discounted household appliances, which provided cash for future projects. After the Fire of 1947, Bun and his family collected stones from the foundations of burned mansions to help build his stone house on Harbor Lane, making it an unofficial monument to the lost houses of the cottage era. His house was built on the burned site of Ann Dennison's Strath-Eden cottage (1894).

After Sonny married Sylvia Young on November 5, 1948, and Jimmy Cough married Mary L. St. Peter on February 4, 1956, both couples began to raise families and needed other sources of income for family expenses and future projects. The Cough brothers' side jobs included moonlighting as a schoolteacher, television repairman, salvage hauler, driving school instructor, school bus driver, scuba diving instructor, county sheriff and bartender. Sonny and Jimmy also started the first sightseeing tour bus company in Bar Harbor, Acadia National Park Tour Bus in 1955.

In 1969, Leslie C. Brewer, Father James Gower, Sonny Cough, Bob Smith, Richard Lewis and others helped establish the College of the Atlantic (COA).[209] Mike and Nettie Garber provided properties purchased from the Oblate Seminary, which included Guy's Cliff (1878) and Turrets (1893).

Additional land and financial backing came from the Cough family, Charlie Sawyer and others. Sea Urchins (1886), Sea Fox (1903), Acadia (Biddle Cottage, 1887) and Witch Cliff (1880) cottages were later acquired and restored along with the other two cottages on the thirty-seven-acre campus. Guy's Cliff burned in 1983 and was replaced with the Kaelber Hall.

The surviving stone circle from the porch of Beau Desert (1882) was used by the Oblate Fathers for the base of the large blue neon cross installed in the 1950s as part of their seminary. In the 1970s, COA students installed a windmill on the stone circle that burned in the 1980s. The Our Lady of Fatima Shrine also survives on the campus. After the college was established, the unrealistic goal of some residents to re-create the Gilded Age estates along Eden Street shore was dead.

Sonny took all that his family learned in business and real estate and took it to the next level with his charisma, vision, community activism and attention to quality. He was active in the town government and other civic groups and eventually allied with other progressive residents in the town who wanted to change zoning in the Gateway district. His approach was practical and nonconfrontational. Although the original zoning plan of 1961 began the process, it took another ten years and the development of the College of the Atlantic as a buffer to gain a consensus that only the

Oblate Cross, Our Lady of Fatima Shrine, 1960s. *Courtesy of the author.*

land nearest the town on Eden Street would remain residential. The new zoning plans moved away from preserving the multi-acre zoning to attract rich taxpayers and allowed land near the ferry terminal to be developed. The Holiday Inn Resort, the Oakes and the Bayview hotels were built under the new zoning.

Oakes Inc. was established after the purchase of the Oakes property in the late 1960s, which added another piece of property on Frenchman Bay under Cough ownership. This property was given to Bowdoin College after the Fire of 1947 by the Oakes family and was used as a conference center for the school called the Oakes Center of Bowdoin. The college was no longer interested in retaining the property in the late 1960s since it was costly to maintain and decided to sell it to the Coughs in 1969.[210]

Sonny loved to tell the story of millionaire Harry Oakes, the most famous owner of the Oakes cottage, the Willows. He recalled that the house was built in 1913 for Charlotte Baker, and after she died, Oakes bought the property in 1940 and was murdered not long after in 1943 in the Bahamas under suspicious circumstances. Sonny opened the Atlantic Oakes by the Sea in the 1970s with the Willows, some added motel units, a pool and tennis courts. When Bun Cough passed in 1978 in Old Town, he had only seen the start of the Cough motel development and the changes to the Gateway district of Bar Harbor.

In 1986, Sony built the Atlantic Eyrie Lodge on the site where the Stanwood cottage (1885) burned in 1947.[211] The cottage was owned by Maine politician James Blaine and later famous composer and conductor Walter Damrosch. The Atlantic Eyrie Lodge is the only Cough-owned hotel still in the town. Daniel Cough's wife, Elvira Higgins, was related to James Blaine through his wife, who was a Stanwood.

In the late 1980s, Bar Harbor began to flourish as a tourist town, and Sonny decided to transform the mansion hotel into a first-class resort hotel. The emergence of Walsh and Witham organizations in the Bar Harbor hotel business during the last twenty years makes the next phase of the development of the Atlantic Oakes seem less important; however, this was a large project at the time, costing about $2 million in the first phase of the project.

The creation of the Bar Harbor Inn in the 1950s provided the model for the development of an existing historical property into a larger hotel. This post-fire project was a community effort to revitalize the status of the aged resort town by transforming the Reading Room into a modern motel. The people involved in the project included all of Bar Harbor's key civic

Sonny Cough in navy uniform, 1945. *Courtesy of the author.*

Armstrong wedding at the Bar Harbor Inn, August 25, 1951, with Otis Armstrong, Quentin E. Armstrong, Constance Ells Armstrong and Venessa Hall McKay. *Courtesy of the author.*

leaders at the time. The architect of the Oakes project, Quentin E. "Monk" Armstrong, and his wife, Constance "Connie" Ells, had their wedding reception at the newly renovated Bar Harbor Inn on August 25, 1951, and Sonny Cough was a guest.

Sonny and Monk were born days apart during the summer of 1927. They both lived through the frugal times during the Great Depression and both joined the navy in 1945 when they turned eighteen and the war was coming to an end. Their military service gave them access to the GI Bill, and both went to college, which provided them with the skills to prosper in the postwar 1950s. Sonny and his wife, Sylvia, were old friends of Monk's wife, Connie Ells.

The Oakes project was very important for Monk since he was an outsider from New Jersey who wanted to develop a private architecture business on Mount Desert Island, which was not easy for a person from "away." The Oakes project launched the next twenty-seven years of his private practice, which ended with the last payment for architecture services a few months before his death in February 2015 at the age of eighty-seven.

Armstrong was a partner in a successful architectural firm in New Jersey, Armstrong Jordan Pease, for twenty years. Although the core business of his firm was the sixty schools they built and renovated, he did work on a few restoration/renovation projects concerning historic buildings such as the Freehold United Methodist Church and nineteenth-century Drumthwacket, the official New Jersey governor's residence. These projects provided experience in renovating older buildings to meet the current needs with modern alterations and additions.

In reviewing the documents associated with the Oakes project that are part of the Quentin E. Armstrong collection at the Maine Historical Society in Portland, the complexity of the construction of the Oakes hotel is apparent.[212] The core of this phase of development was the four-story building with two sailboats on the front that transformed the property into a visual gateway to Bar Harbor. The second phase of the project in the early 2000s added the conference center. After the design phase was completed, the zoning and approvals process took several months to complete to get the necessary permits. The completion of this phase of the project must have been a feeling of triumph for Sonny considering all the obstacles his family faced with zoning with other Gateway district projects.

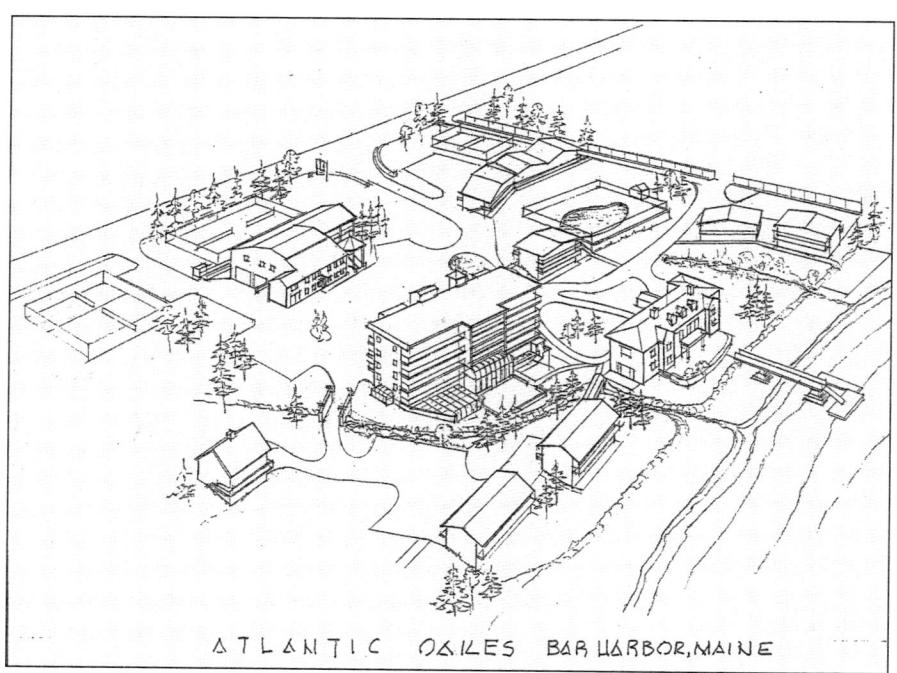

Expansion plan (early 1990s) drawing of the Atlantic Oakes by the Sea (aka Atlantic Oceanside Hotel and Conference Center) at 119 Eden Street. *Courtesy of the author.*

Key to Sonny's design was the preservation of the Willows. He wanted the hotel to reflect Bar Harbor's past, present and future. An estate on Frenchman Bay that was once for a small group of wealthy people to enjoy became available to middle-class families. Although some preservation purists criticized the renovation, the Atlantic Oakes was a commercial property, not a private residence or public building. Some of the renovation decisions reflected the seasonal nature of the business and the harsh winters. The construction of the attic suite (now called deluxe penthouse) in the Willows created premium lodging in the original building. The suite changed the original roof design; however, it also provided another room with a spectacular view of Frenchman Bay.

The Bar Harbor Ferry Terminal was a key factor in the development of the Oakes property. Before the cruise ships began to come frequently to the town, the ferry to Nova Scotia was a key transposition hub and placed the hotel in an excellent location. Sonny was on the local committee that convinced the CNR (Canadian National Railroad) in the 1950s to add Bar Harbor as a port of entry in the United States. Sonny and Jimmy Cough considered hotel and tourist services for ferry visitors a priority.

The design phase of the four-story hotel project called Oakes New Motel/Center began in the fall of 1988, and final close out was in March 1991. The new building included an indoor pool, year-round office, breakfast room and laundry room. A conference center was added later that had at least four additions. The two-story conference center was an important addition to the property since Bar Harbor needed modern meeting rooms in the early 2000s. The conference center was also used for weekly lobster bakes provided by Sonny's son Steve and daughter-in-law Ann Cough for a number of years during the summer months before they constructed their own building in Hulls Cove for the dinners.

After Jimmy died in 2002 and Sonny in 2007,[213] the family continued to manage the Oakes. In 2008, the Witham family purchased 150-room Atlantic Oakes, situated on approximately seven hundred feet of oceanfront with eight distinctive guest buildings, as well as conference facilities that accommodate eight hundred people.[214] They changed the name of the hotel to the Atlantic Oceanside Hotel and Event Center. Over the next ten years of ownership, the Witham Family Limited Partnership made extensive renovations to the property. Their hotel is now called a "153-room, 3-star hotel" that "welcomes guests with free breakfast, a private beach, and an outdoor pool."[215] The Willows mansion was completely restored in 2008.

Monk Armstrong's other large design projects in town included the Lisa Stewart Women's Health Center for Joe Cough and renovation of the Mira Monte Inn and Suites for Marian Burns. Other commercial projects that he worked on alone or with Moore and Associates included Bar Harbor Bike Shop, Town Hill Market/Store, Village Green/Carmen Veranda Restaurant, Galyn's Restaurant, Rosalie's Pizza, Thirsty Whale Restaurant and the Dog and Pony Tavern and Restaurant. He provided design work for the following hotels/inns: Holland Inn, Central House, Golden Anchor Motel, Bayview Hotel, Briarwood Inn and the Grey Rock Inn.

Another Cough-owned hotel, the twenty-six-room Bayview Hotel (111 Eden Street), built in 1985, was located on the site of Bournemouth (aka Burnmouth, 1896), which was torn down in 1979. The oceanfront property also included a fifty-seat restaurant and six townhouses with ocean views. The Bayview, sold to Kim Swan in 2019, was another property developed when the zoning changed.

Sonny and Sylvia Cough originally had a house on the grounds of the Oakes property before Monk helped Sonny design a house on Norman Drive overlooking the Oakes and the College of the Atlantic. Mossley Hall (1883), one of the grandest Bar Harbor mansions, was once located on the same property. The estate was razed in the 1940s; however, Sonny incorporated a surviving retaining wall from the old building into the landscaping of the new house, which reflected his connection to the town's history.

The Cough family history on Mount Desert Island is a great immigrant success story. Daniel Cough's humble beginning could not have foretold the future of his descendants. His great-grandson Sonny Cough has been called "Bar Harbor's first hotel mogul";[216] however, he is instead part of the pantheon of hotel giants, including the Brewers, the Robertses, the Hamors, the Rodicks and all those Higginses, that provided memorable accommodations to visitors of the island over the years. As people look from their hotel balconies from any of the hotels on the island today, they cannot help but be reminded of Jane Parker's question in 1916 that is as relevant to the Gilded Age millionaire rusticator as it is to the twenty-first-century tourist: "Where could be found more beauty, more charm, more mystery, than on the Island of Mount Desert?"

Bonus Historical Sites: The How Memorial by William Ordway Partridge in How Park (behind the Wonder View Inn on Cleftstone Road) commemorates the life of Chas. T. How (1840–1909), a lawyer and real estate developer from Boston who launched the mansion development era of Bar Harbor, selling the land where great mansions such as Blair Eyrie (1888), Mizzentop (1884), Stanwood (1886) and the Turrets (1893) were built. He is also credited with the first land donation to the future Acadia National Park when he donated Fawn Pond to the BHVIA in 1906.

Sonogee (131 Eden Street, 1903), the estate owned by Henry Lane Eno, Lyman Kendall, Frederick Vanderbilt, A. Atwater Kent and Richard Wetzel before becoming a rehabilitation and senior living center, is now owned by Ocean Properties.

AFTERWORD

July 1969 was one of the last times I saw my grandfather Dr. John B. Ells. We were vacationing in Maine, and the town was filled with the sights and sounds of the '60s: long hair, rock music and teenage rebellion. Grandpa was kind of a fish out of water in this era. After all, he was a teetotaling veteran from the First World War born during the Victorian era trying to make sense of the drug culture, the sexual revolution and the antiwar movement. As we drove around that day, my sister, Janice, was sitting in Agamont Park near the fountain with some longhaired male companions. Grandpa was jealous that his granddaughter had interests other than him and said with his usual stutter, "What do those guys have that I don't have?" As I looked over at the bald octogenarian, I said, "Hair, Grandpa, hair." He roared with laughter because he always enjoyed a joke on himself.

Later that day, we went up to his apartment at 68½ Main Street in the Bar Harbor Times Building to watch the Apollo 11 moon landing. This building was razed a few decades ago and replaced with Ben and Bill's Chocolate Emporium (66 Main Street). I have the coat rack that visitors saw as they climbed up the steps to Dr. Ells's dentist office. As kid, I used to love watching the July 4 parade from the bay windows overlooking Main Street.

For my generation, the moon landing was just another step in the goal of space travel and technological progress. But to John B. Ells, the landing on the moon was the unthinkable. Here was a man whose college job was removing horse excrement from the streets of Bar Harbor, and now he was looking at the ultimate human technological achievement. He stared at

Afterword

Dr. John B. Ells sitting on the wharf bench in the 1960s. *Courtesy of the author.*

the images transmitted from space in awe. His old friend, Maine senator Margaret Chase Smith, was a strong supporter of NASA. Dr. James Webb, NASA director, said that without her help "we never would have placed a man on the moon." To me, that moment summed up what a long and interesting journey had occurred for Bar Harbor and his generation during the previous eighty years. They experienced some of the best and worst moments of American history, survived and prospered.

It is only fitting that I end this book at the wharf that Dr. Ells loved so much and was so important to the history of the town. It was here that he regularly caught three flounders on one hook fishing and convened his nightly meetings of the "wharf rats." On a foggy night, it is not hard to imagine his spirit being joined by Tobias Roberts and others on the wharf waiting for the ghost ship the MV *Bluenose* to come from behind the Porcupine Islands as they look out to sea to welcome the sailors, ships, rusticators and visitors of the world to the tiny town of Bar Harbor. They knew what a gem the town was and that those who visited would never forget the experience.

NOTES

Chapter 1

1. Sherman, *Sherman's Bar Harbor Guide*, 66.
2. *New York Times*, August 6, 1899.
3. Ibid.
4. Ibid.
5. Walsh, "Pier a Rock-Solid Memorial to Dr. John Ells," G2.
6. Ibid.
7. Ibid.
8. Ibid.
9. *Bar Harbor Times*, August 16, 1973.
10. Sherman, *Sherman's Bar Harbor Guide*, 82.
11. *Lewiston [ME] Daily Sun*, July 12, 1906, 16.
12. Ibid.
13. *Bar Harbor Record*, October 11, 1905, 1.
14. *Leslie's*, March 4, 1888, 395.
15. Messer, *History of the Bar Harbor Inn*, 72–73.
16. Ibid.
17. *Bar Harbor Times*, April 10, 1947, p. 1.
18. Ibid., August 11, 1949, 13.
19. Ibid.
20. *Maine, University of Maine General Alumni Association Magazine* 76, no. 1 (Spring/Summer 1995): 30–32.

Chapter 2

21. *Lewiston [ME] Evening Journal*, August 15, 1923, 1, 3.
22. *Bar Harbor Times*, August 3, 1932, 1.
23. Ibid., August 31, 1932, 8.
24. Ibid.
25. Ibid., July 7, 1933, 3; July 12, 1933, 2.
26. Ibid.
27. Ibid., June 28, 1935, 1, 4.
28. Ibid.
29. Ibid.
30. Ibid.
31. Ibid.
32. Ibid., May 15, 1936, 2.
33. Ibid., June 2, 1936, 6.

Chapter 3

34. Unknown Arkansas newspaper.
35. Ibid.
36. *Bar Harbor Times*, November 25, 1925, 3.

Chapter 4

37. Bar Harbor Village Improvement Association, "History," barharborvia.org/about-us/history.
38. Ibid.
39. Originally broadcast in 1971 by Ernest Marriner on the 1000th episode of his radio show, *Little Talks*, in Waterville, Maine.
40. Ibid.
41. *Bar Harbor Record*, May 4, 1904, 1.

Chapter 5

42. *Bar Harbor Mount Desert Herald*, June 23, 1882, 3.

Chapter 6

43. Crawford, *Old Bar Harbor*, 84.
44. *Bar Harbor Record*, July 4, 1906, 9.

Chapter 7

45. *Bar Harbor Times*, February 13, 1929, 1, 8.
46. Vandenbergh and Shettleworth, *Opulence to Ashes*, 41.
47. *Bar Harbor Record*, September 19, 1906, 8.
48. *Bar Harbor Times*, February 20, 1929, 1, 8.

Chapter 8

49. Ibid., July 6, 1939, 4; June 22, 1939, 4; June 29, 1939, 4.

Chapter 9

50. CPI Inflation Calculator, www.in2013dollars.com/1882-dollars-in-2019.
51. Maine Maritime Museum, Bath, ME, list of vessel owners and captains.
52. Captain Ash from P. Pineo (HCCO Book 80/Page 379), January 12, 1847, $1,000.
53. Mystic Seaport, Mystic, CT, list of vessel owners and captains. (www.mysticseaport.org)
54. Penobscot Marine Museum, Searsport, ME, list of vessel owners and captains.
55. Hale, *Story of Bar Harbor*, 121.
56. United States congressional serial set inventory control record 3, issue 4978, *Merchant Sailing Vessels of the United States*, 141.
57. *Bar Harbor Mount Desert Herald*, May 17, 1883, 2.
58. Maine Maritime Museum, Bath, ME, list of ships.
59. Chris Costa, "Black History in Maine: Was Acadia's Frazer Point Named for the Firsr Documented, Free Black Resident of the Area?" New Center Maine, February 18, 2021, www.newscentermaine.com/article/news/local/black-history/black-history-in-maine-acadias-frazer-point-could-be-named-for-the-first-documented-free-black-resident/97-6b0c9189-711d-461e-aac6-15574aa60bd5.
60. Ibid.

61. Bolster, *Black Jacks*, 19, Black Jacks photo/drawing insert page in the center of book, caption for drawing of Captain Absalom Boston.
62. John Golden, volunteer researcher, Stephen Phillips Memorial Library, Penobscot Marine Museum, Searsport, ME.
63. *Bar Harbor Times*, May 29, 1915, 5.

Chapter 10

64. Vandenbergh and Shettleworth, *Opulence to Ashes*, 105.
65. David E. Higgins posting of the biography of Carolyn E. Higgins written by his cousins Gail and Brenda Webber.
66. Moseley Cottage Inn & Town Motel, "Moseley Cottage Inn History," moseleycottage.net/2016/04/07/moseley-cottage-inn-history.
67. *Bar Harbor Record*, March 23, 1898, 1.
68. Ibid., April 11, 1900, 12.
69. Special Collections, Raymond H. Fogler Library, University of Maine, "Higgins (Edward Leander) Architectural Records, 1910-1951" (2016). Finding Aids. Number 274.https://digitalcommons.library.umaine.edu/findingaids/274.

Chapter 11

70. Ibid., April 24, 1901, 5.
71. Sweetser, *Kings Handbook of Newton*, 82–84.
72. *Newton Graphic*, July 11, 1948; July 22, 1948; *Boston Globe*, July 23, 1948.
73. Mary Shannon Journal, Newton Collection.
74. *Wabash [IN] Courier* 24, no. 34, April 12, 1856, lists his divorce case.
75. Cheney, *Reminiscences of Ednah Dow Cheney*, 53–56.
76. Ibid.
77. Ibid.
78. Cowan's, "Mary Shannon, Boston Abolitionist and Women's Rights Activist, Collection Featuring Photos, Letter, and Wood from John Brown's Gallows," www.cowanauctions.com/lot/mary-shannon-boston-abolitionist-and-women-s-rights-activist-collection-featuring-photos-letter-and-wood-from-john-brown-s-gallows-3229204.
79. Rebecca Pomroy Foundation, "Who We Are," www.pomroy.org/who-we-are.
80. Ibid.

81. *Bar Harbor Record*, November 29, 1888, 5.
82. Ibid., May 4, 1904, 1.
83. *Bar Harbor Mount Desert Herald*, October 8, 1881, 2.
84. Ibid., October 26, 1882, 3.
85. *Bar Harbor Record*, September 16, 1903, 8; September 13, 1888, 4.
86. Booker T. Washington Papers, vol. 2: 1860–89, letter from Mary C. Shannon to Book T. Washington, January 1887, books.google.com/books?isbn=025200243.
87. *Bar Harbor Record*, April 24, 1901, 4, 5.
88. Ibid.
89. Ibid.

Chapter 12

90. *Bar Harbor Times*, January 13, 1932, 1.
91. McLane, *Islands of the Mid-Maine Coast*, 135–36.
92. *Bar Harbor Mount Desert Herald*, August 17, 1881, 3.
93. Charles H. Berry and Fred H. Berry to Edward Samuel (HCCO Deed Book 200/page 481), September 15, 1885.
94. *Bar Harbor Record*, October 23, 1895.
95. Ibid., March 27, 1896, 1.
96. Zenobia Grant Wingate, "Albert Gallatin," Caldwell Gallery, www.caldwellgallery.com/artists/albert-eugene-gallatin/biography.
97. Vallarino Fine Art, "Albert Eugene Gallatin," www.vallarinofineart.com/albert-e-gallatin.
98. Gallatin, *Art and the Great War*.
99. *Ellsworth American*, May 22, 1879.

Chapter 13

100. Central Maine, "Maine's Forgotten Dead," May 26, 2012, www.centralmaine.com/2012/05/27/maines-forgotten-dead_2012-05-26.
101. *Bar Harbor Mount Desert Herald*, December 17, 1881, 2.
102. Ibid., April 24, 1885, 3.
103. *Bar Harbor Record*, February 7, 1906, 5.
104. Ibid., April 11, 1906, 5.
105. *The Islander* 7, no. 2 (December 1915).

106. Dunnack, *Maine Book*, 273, 274.
107. State of Maine Department of Health and Human Services, "About Riverview," www.maine.gov/dhhs/riverview/history/timeline.html.

Chapter 14

108. Benjamin Ash to Mariah Ash (HCCO Deed Book 163/page 228), October 15, 1878.
109. *Bar Harbor Mount Desert Herald*, September 9, 1887, 4.

Chapter 15

110. *Bar Harbor Record*, December 22, 1887, 5.
111. Ibid., February 27, 1895, 9.
112. Ibid.
113. Ibid.
114. Ibid.
115. *Bar Harbor Times*, May 27, 1925, 4.
116. Ibid., February 28, 1952, 2.
117. *Bar Harbor Record*, January 30, 1901, 5.
118. *Bar Harbor Times*, February 8, 1951, 1, 10.
119. *Bar Harbor Record*, March 1, 1911, 5.
120. Ibid., February 25, 1914, 5.
121. Ibid.
122. *Bar Harbor Times*, January 13, 1917, 5.
123. Maine Memory Network, "Mount Desert Island: Shaped by Nature, Basketball: From Rivals to Teammates," mdi.mainememory.net/page/3758/display.html.
124. Information from Debbie Dyer from the Bar Harbor Historical Society.
125. *Bar Harbor Record*, "Brilliant Ball," February 20, 1895, 1.
126. Ibid.
127. Ibid.
128. *Bar Harbor Times*, March 15, 1919, 1.

Chapter 16

129. Karen M. Starko, "Salicylates and Pandemic Influenza Mortality, 1918–1919, Pharmacology, Pathology and Historic Evidence," Oxford Academic, November 15, 2009, academic.oup.com/cid/article/49/9/1405/301441/Salicylates-and-Pandemic-Influenza-Mortality-1918.
130. *Bar Harbor Times*, October 19, 1918, 5.
131. Ibid., October 5, 1918, 1.

Chapter 17

132. *Bar Harbor Record*, June 20, 1900, 5.
133. Ibid., November 6, 1907, 5.
134. Ibid., June 24, 1914, 5.
135. *Bar Harbor Times*, July 16, 1924, 5.
136. Ibid.
137. Ibid.
138. Ibid., 38–39.
139. Ibid., 40.
140. Ibid., January 20, 1926, 6.
141. Ibid.
142. Ibid., January 16, 1929, 1.
143. Ibid., March 19, 1930, 1.
144. Ibid.
145. Ibid., July 9, 1930, 1.
146. Ibid.
147. Ibid., September 14, 1932, 1.
148. Ibid., October 6, 1938, 1; November 24, 1938, 1.
149. Ibid., February 23, 1939, 2.
150. Ibid., August 30, 1956, 14.
151. Ibid., April 30, 1959, 1.
152. Ibid., September 3, 1959, 1.

Chapter 18

153. *Bar Harbor Record*, June 7, 1894, 1.
154. *The Courier* (Lincoln, NE), August 17, 1895, 11.

155. Ibid.
156. Ibid.
157. *Bar Harbor Record*, November 18, 1896, 5.
158. Ibid., July 28, 1897, 9.
159. Ibid., November 2, 1898, 6.
160. *Medical Council*, vol. 13, January 1908.
161. Ibid.
162. *Bar Harbor Record*, June 15, 1910, 5.
163. Ibid.
164. *Ellsworth American*, "Lorenzo Cavanaugh Creamer Jr. Obituary," May 22, 2012.

Chapter 19

165. *The Atlantic Reporter*, vol. 38, 554–55.
166. Sherman, *Sherman's Bar Harbor Guide*, 26.
167. Ibid.
168. *Chicago Tribune*, April 28, 1888, 3; *New York Times*, May 4, 1888; *People's Press* (Winston-Salem, NC), May 3, 1888, 2.
169. Tolles, *Summer by the Seaside*, 170.
170. *Bar Harbor Record*, January 10, 1900, 5.
171. This Old Wood, www.thisoldwood.com.
172. *Bar Harbor Record*, January 10, 1900, 5.
173. Ibid., October 30, 1907, 1.
174. Ibid., August 29, 1906, 5.
175. Ibid., January 17, 1900, 5.
176. Cultural Landscape Foundation, "Ottawa Park," tclf.org/landscapes/ottawa-park.
177. Ibid.
178. *Chamber of Commerce Journal of Maine* 23 (1910): 25.
179. *Maine Reports* 115 (1917): 507–13.
180. Yetter, *Bar Harbor in the Roaring Twenties*, 100–2.
181. Lynn Sweet, "Obama's Day and Date Night in Bar Harbor, Maine," July 18, 2010, blogs.suntimes.com/sweet/2010/07/obamas_day_and_date_night_in_b.html; Michael Memoli, "The Obama Family in Maine," *Tribune Washington Bureau*, July 17, 2010.
182. Mount Desert Island, "Golden Years," mountdesertisland.net/goldenyears.html.

183. New York Social Diary, "Vanderbilts Under the Pines," www.newyorksocialdiary.com/the-way-they-live/2011/vanderbilts-under-the-pines.
184. *Bangor Daily News*, June 25, 1981, 76.
185. Harborside Hotel website and brochure.
186. Sweet, "Obama's Day and Night."

Chapter 20

187. Currier, "Greeter of the Fleets," 18–23, 49–50
188. Ibid.
189. Ibid.
190. Ibid.
191. Ibid.
192. Ibid.
193. *Bar Harbor Record*, June 21, 1905, 5.
194. La Rochelle Mansion and Museum, barharborhistorical.org.

Chapter 21

195. *Bar Harbor Mount Desert Herald*, October 15, 1886, 4.
196. Ibid., April 1, 1887, 3.
197. *Bar Harbor Record*, April 14, 1887, 1.
198. Ibid., October 31, 1889, 4.
199. Ibid.
200. Ibid.
201. Ibid.
202. Ibid., December 1, 1892, 1.
203. Ibid., July 10, 1907, 5.
204. Ibid.
205. Ibid.
206. *Bar Harbor Times*, September 11, 1929, 2.
207. Ibid., August 20, 1942, 1.

Chapter 22

208. Zwicker and Zwicker, *Whitemarsh Hall*, 81.
209. COA Magazine 2, no. 1 (Winter 2006), issuu.com/collegeoftheatlantic/docs/coamagazine_winter06_orgnl.
210. Maine Memory Network, "The Willows, Bar Harbor, ca. 1920," www.mainememory.net/artifact/25016.
211. Dyer, *Bar Harbor: A Town Almost Lost*, 11.
212. Atlantic Oakes by the Sea/Song of the Sea Apt (today called Atlantic Oceanside Hotel & Event Center), (1988–2005), 119 Eden Street, Bar Harbor, ME 04609. Drawings: 40. Files: 38 (13 drawings in file, box 2), (25 drawings in box 1).
213. *Ellsworth American*, "James Cough Obituary," April 11, 2002, ellsworthamerican.com/archive/obit2002/04-02/ea_obit13_04-11-02.html; *Bangor Daily News*, "Bernard K. 'Sonny' Cough," September 25, 2008, available at Southwest Harbor Public Library, swhplibrary.net/digitalarchive/files/original/3009/Cough_-_Bernard_K._Cough.pdf.
214. Bill Trotter, "Bar Harbor Hotelier Buys Two More Motels," *Bangor Daily News*, September 18, 2001, bangordailynews.com/2010/09/18/business/bar-harbor-hotelier-buys-two-more-motels/.
215. Orbitz, "Atlantic Oceanside Hotel & Conference Center," www.orbitz.com/Bar-Harbor-Hotels-Atlantic-Oceanside-Hotel-Conference-Center.h24093.Hotel-Information.
216. *Bangor Daily News*, "Bernard K. 'Sonny' Cough."

BIBLIOGRAPHY

Articles

Chilman, C. William. "Farewell to a Golden Time." *Down East Magazine*, January 1969, 38–40, 45.

Currier, Isabel. "Greeter of the Fleets." *Down East Magazine*, March 1962, 18.

Downeast Scenic Railroad. "A Brief History of the Maine Shore Line Railroad/The Maine Central Railroad Bar Harbor Branch, Now the Home of the Downeast Scenic Railroad." www.downeastscenicrail.org/ride/about/history.

Hornsby, Stephen J. "The Gilded Age and the Making of Bar Harbor." *Geographical Review* 83, no. 4 (October 1993): 455–68.

Pritchard, Becky. "Schools and Businesses Closed to Prevent Virus Spread a Hundred Years Ago." *Mount Desert Islander*, March 26, 2020, 1. www.mdislander.com/maine-news/schools-and-businesses-closed-to-prevent-virus-spread-a-hundred-years-ago.

Shannon, Mary. Mary Shannon Journal, Newton Collection. www.newtonma.gov/gov/historic/research/collections/papers/shannon.asp.

Books

Boardman Crowninshield Bradlee, Francis. *The Eastern Railroad: A Historical Account of Early Railroading in Eastern New England*. Salem, MA: Essex Institute, 1922.

Bibliography

Bolster, W. Jeffrey. *Black Jacks: African American Seamen in the Age of Sail*. Cambridge, MA: Harvard Press, 1997.

Cheney, Ednah Dow Littlehale. *Reminiscences of Ednah Dow Cheney (Born Littlehale)*. Boston: Lee & Shepard, 1902. www.archive.org/stream/reminiscencesofe00chenuoft/reminiscencesofe00chenuoft_djvu.txt.

Crawford, F. Marion. *Old Bar Harbor: A Walk Down Main Street*. New York: Charles Scribner and Sons, 1894.

Dunnack, Henry E. *The Maine Book*. Augusta: Librarian of Maine State Library, 1920.

Dyer, Deborah M. *Bar Harbor: A Town Almost Lost: A Pictorial Essay of Bar Harbor's Mansions Before and After the Fire*. Bar Harbor, ME: self-published, 2008.

Fox, Barbara Merrill. *Lest We Forget: Band Stands of Maine: An Illustrated History*. Bar Harbor, ME: Foxrun Associates, 2003.

Gallatin, Albert Eugene. *Art and the Great War*. Boston: E.P. Dutton, 1919.

Hale, Richard W., Jr. *The Story of Bar Harbor*. New York: Ives Washburn Inc., 1949.

Helfrich, G.W., and Gladys O'Neil. *Lost Bar Harbor*. Camden, ME: Down East Books, 1982.

Hill, Ruth Ann. *Discovering Old Bar Harbor and Acadia National Park: An Unconventional History and Guide*. Camden, ME: Down East Books, 1993.

McBride, Bunny, and Harald E.L. Prins. *Indians in Eden: Wabanakis and Rusticators on Maine's Mt. Desert Island*. Camden, ME: Down East Books, 2009.

McLane, Charles B. *Islands of the Mid-Maine Coast*. Falmouth, ME: Kennebec River Press, 1989.

Messer, Vincent C. *A History of the Bar Harbor Inn*. Bar Harbor, ME: Vincent C. Messer, 2010.

Morrison, Samuel Eliot. *The Story of Mount Desert Island*. Boston: Little, Brown, and Company, 1960.

Sherman, W.H. *Sherman's Bar Harbor Guide, Business Directory and Reference Book (1890)*. Bar Harbor, ME: Bar Harbor Press Co., 1890.

Shettleworth, Earle G., Jr. *Bar Harbor: Postcard History Series*. Charleston, SC: Arcadia Publishing, 2011.

Street, George E., edited by Samuel A. Eliot. *Mount Desert: A History*. Boston: Houghton Mifflin Company, 1905, revised 1926.

Sweetser, M.F. *Chisholm's Mount Desert Guide Book*. Portland, ME: Chisholm Brothers, 1888, 1900.

———. *Kings Handbook of Newton, Mass*. Boston: Moses King Corporation, 1889.

Bibliography

Tolles, Bryant Franklin. *Summer by the Seaside: The Architecture of New England Coastal Resort Hotels*. Lebanon, NH: University Press of New England, 2008.

Turner, Loretta M. *When Bar Harbor Was Eden*. Charleston, SC: Arcadia Publishing, 1995.

Vandenbergh, Lydia Bodman, and Earle G. Shettleworth Jr. *Opulence to Ashes: Bar Harbor's Gilded Century, 1850–1950*. Camden, ME: Down East Enterprise Inc., 2009.

Yetter, Luann. *Bar Harbor in the Roaring Twenties: From Village Life to the High Life on Mount Desert Island*. Charleston, SC: The History Press, 2015.

Zwicker, Charles G., and Edward C. Zwicker. Whitemarsh Hall: The Estate of Edward T. Stotesbury. Charleston, SC: Arcadia Publishing, 2004.

Newspapers

Numerous newspaper articles and items from the *Bar Harbor Mount Desert Herald*, *Bar Harbor Record* and the *Bar Harbor Times* were referenced for this book. Cottage listings were usually included on page 2 or 3 of the newspapers except for the *Bar Harbor Mount Desert Herald*, which sometimes included the listing on the front page. Most articles were on the front page or in local items page (usually on pages 4–6). Direct quotes are cited in the notes.

Bangor [ME] Daily News, June 25, 1981, 76.
Bangor [ME] Daily Whig and Courier, February 22, 1895.
Boston Globe, September 26, 1897.
Chicago Tribune, April 28, 1888.
The Courier (Lincoln, NE), August 17, 1895.
Ellsworth American (Hancock County, ME), May 22, 1879.
———, July 30, 1896.
———, November 11, 1897.
Leslie's 65–67 by Frank Leslie, March 4, 1888.
Lewiston [ME] Daily Sun, July 12, 1906.
Lewiston [ME] Evening Journal, October 2, 1912.
———, August 15, 1923.
Lewiston [ME] Evening Press, September 27, 1897.
Make, Liz. "Opinion: Chinese-on-the-Inside." *New York Times*, March 3, 2014.
Nashua [NH] Telegraph, December 13, 1971.

BIBLIOGRAPHY

New York Times, May 4, 1888.
——, August 6, 1899.
——, July 11, 1976.
People's Press (Winston-Salem, NC), May 3, 1888.
Portsmouth [NH] Herald, May 13, 1952, 10, navy citation.
Wabash [IN] Courier 24, no. 34, April 12, 1856.
Walsh, David. "Pier a Rock-Solid Memorial to Dr. John Ells." *Bangor Daily News*, June 30, 2001, G2.

ABOUT THE AUTHOR

Brian Armstrong with his wife, Rose, in Bar Harbor. *Courtesy of the author.*

Brian Armstrong was born in Flemington, New Jersey, and grew up in Stanton, New Jersey. He received a bachelor's degree in history and political science from American University in Washington, D.C. He lives now in Mount Laurel, New Jersey.

Armstrong worked for forty years for various technology and staffing companies, including EDS, Kelly Services and International Technology Solutions, Inc.

He was president of the South River Historical and Preservation Society for ten years and is now the vice president, Central Region, for the League of Historical Societies of New Jersey.

He is an independent historian, researcher and author. In 2015, he cowrote the Arcadia book *South River* with Stephanie Bartz and Nan Whitehead. Armstrong authored The History Press book *The Franklin Park Tragedy: A Forgotten Story of Racial Injustice in New Jersey* in 2019 and won the NJSAA Author Award for the book in 2020. He also frequently writes articles for the

About the Author

Bar Harbor Historical Society in Bar Harbor, Maine, where his mother's family lived for several hundred years.

Mr. Armstrong lectures on local history, World War I, the Spanish influenza and political history. He is a collector of U.S. presidential election memorabilia and is a member of American Political Items Collectors (APIC).

Armstrong is married to Rosemarie Rufo Armstrong and is father of two daughters and one grandson.

Visit us at
www.historypress.com